The Inferno

THE INFERNO
- O F -
DANTE ALIGHIERI

A MODERN ENGLISH EDITION

BY ETHAN C. JAHNS

ARTWORK
BY LEA RATZMANN

This book is dedicated to my family and friends, who have found it in their hearts to show me an exceptional amount of tolerance in all my pursuits.

«Omai convien che tu così ti spoltre,»
disse 'l maestro, «ché seggendo in piuma
in fama non si vien, né sotto coltre;

sanza la qual chi sua vita consuma,
cotal vestigio in terra di sé lascia
qual fummo in aere e in acqua la schiuma.»

"From this point on, you must put off your laziness," my master said, "for men do not find fame while on cushions or under bed sheets;

and anyone who lives his life fameless leaves his legacy like smoke in the air or foam on water."

Inferno 24.46-51

Contents

PREFACE

When I undertook the writing of this book, I was motivated by one question: "Shouldn't there be a translation of Dante's *Inferno* that is more suited to the average reader?" I saw two problems with most translations in regard to this question. The first was that the style and word choice of the translations were confusing or too lofty for the average reader. The second was that the translator's notes were either few and far between, leaving the reader in confusion, or far more extensive than would be useful or interesting for the average reader (and I confess that I often was tempted to gloss over paragraphs-long notes written over a single line of text).

Accordingly, my approach has been two-fold. In translating I have kept quite close to a literal translation at times, and at other times have deviated quite far from the original, choosing what I felt was most effective for each line. In writing the notes I have done my best to present enough information to fill in the gaps, without saying more than is necessary, though I often go further in-depth on some of the more interesting or significant myths or stories. Above all, this edition is intended as a kind of introductory translation; this should not be the end of your contact with the *Inferno,* but the beginning. For this reason the line numbering in the book corresponds to the original Italian text, so that you can easily reference the text and notes of other translations (many of which use line numbering from the Italian text) to gain more information. It is my hope that this translation will allow you to begin to understand this great piece of literature.

I began this translation toward the end of September 2010, so it was fitting that I finished late in July 2013, 34 months after I had begun (as the *Inferno* has 34 cantos). Along the way many people have been involved directly or indirectly, and I owe them all thanks. I would first like to thank my family, who have supported me with this obsession and allowed me to think aloud for hours on end. I owe a special thanks to my mother, Ann, who volunteered her time to proofread the book to help ensure a professional finish. I also thank my many friends who helped by reading over sections of the book and providing feedback on how to make improvements. There are too many to name, but I especially thank Martin and Michael Loescher for reviewing large sections of the book during the final revisions. I am also greatly indebted to Martin and Michael, as well as my father, Thad, for helping with much of the work of the bookbinding process. I also thank Lea Ratzmann for providing artwork for the title page, an element that definitely brings the book to the next level. Finally, I want to thank you, the reader, without whom this project would not have been possible.

–Ethan C. Jahns

INTRODUCTION

The *Inferno* is the first third of Dante Alighieri's most significant work, the *Divine Comedy*. To understand the *Inferno*, however, we must first familiarize ourselves with the complicated political situation of Dante's time. Dante was born in the year 1265 in the city of Florence in Italy. By this time, Florence was one of the most influential cities in the world: The currency of Florence, the *florin*, was a kind of universal currency, much as the U.S. dollar is in modern times. However, Florence also suffered from severe political unrest. Two political parties, the Guelfs and Ghibellines, had developed in northern and central Italy, and their struggle for power was incredibly prominent in Florence. The division had arisen from disagreements beginning in the 1000s over the power of the Holy Roman Emperor and the Pope. Around the year 1250, those who sided with the interests of the Emperor came to be known as Ghibellines, and those who sided with the Pope known as Guelfs. These two parties were constantly fighting for control of Florence. In the year 1289, however, the Guelfs succeeded in driving the Ghibellines out of Florence after the battles of Campaldino and Caprona (Dante fought in both).

The victory was not long-lasting, however, as the Guelf party itself began to split. Eventually two distinct parties developed, the White Guelfs and Black Guelfs. As a White who had married the daughter of a prominent Black (before the split occurred), Dante was deeply embroiled in the politics of the day. He was elected to several political positions, and in 1300 became one of six priors, the leaders of the city, for one term of two months. During this time the fighting between the Blacks and Whites grew violent, with the Whites wanting more independence for Florence, and the Blacks wanting the Pope to have more control. In 1295, a new Pope, Boniface VIII, had been consecrated. In hopes that Boniface would be able to bring some peace to Florence, embassies were sent to Rome in 1300 and 1301 to gain help from Boniface. Dante was involved in at least one of these embassies. However, Boniface had secretly sided with the Blacks, and in 1301, while Dante was away from Florence, Boniface sent Charles of Valois, the brother of the King of France, to Florence as a "peace-keeper." Charles aided the Blacks in overthrowing the Whites, and Dante was accused of various false charges. When he did not respond to these accusations, he was exiled, and condemned to be burned at the stake should he ever return to Florence. (Interestingly, Florence did not lift the exile until 2008.) Various failed attempts by the Whites to regain power led Dante to abandon the party altogether. For the rest of his life, Dante traveled throughout Italy, living with various politicians and writing. It was probably around 1307 or 1308 that Dante began work on the *Divine Comedy*.

In the *Inferno* the reader will come across the names of many people, places, and events. The many people in Hell come from a variety of places; some are characters from Roman and Greek mythology, some are historical figures, and some were Italians from Dante's time. It must be noted that *Inferno* would have been considered "controversial" in many ways; in it Dante finds in Hell many people who were only recently deceased and still had living immediate family. It is even possible that one of the souls he finds in Hell may have been alive when the *Divine Comedy* was published. Above all, the reader finds Dante largely frustrated with the political situation in Florence. He mentions many political figures from the Ghibellines as well as the White and Black Guelfs. Overall, Dante constructs a complex commentary of his world, which, some 700 years later, can be difficult to interpret.

The *Divine Comedy* stands out as perhaps the greatest single work of all time. Hardly any other work has been so thoroughly studied, translated, and debated. But if we would want to know what the purpose of the *Comedy* is, then we should first read what Dante said in a letter to Can Grande della Scala, his patron: "One would say, briefly, that the goal...is to remove those living in this life from a state of misery, and to lead them to a state of happiness." The purpose, above all, is to lead the reader from a life of sin to a life lived for God.

C A N T O   I

1 Halfway through the journey of our life, I awoke in a dark forest, for I had departed from the straight path.

4 O, how can I even begin to describe what the forest was like, for it was terrible and horrid; even now I cannot think about it without fear taking me again, for this wood was awful,

7 even more than death itself. Nevertheless, because my journey through it yielded a great reward, I will record here the things I saw in that wood.

10 I cannot say how I ended up there, for I was so drowsy when I left the straight path.

13 But when I had reached the edge of the forest I found the foot of a mountain,

16 and looking up I saw the sun's rays, which show all men the right way, coming over the mountain.

19 This light removed some of my fear, which had been in my heart all through that night that had tortured me.

22 And, just as a sailor who has escaped a treacherous sea by reaching shore looks again at the water that had nearly killed him,

so my soul, which still was escaping, looked back over that   25
pass which no man has ever left alive.

After I rested awhile, I resumed my journey up the steep   28
slope so quickly that each step rose above the last.

But see! At the base of the mountain there was a swift and   31
spotted panther!

And as I walked, it constantly blocked my path, so that many   34
times I considered going back to the woods.

This all happened at the beginning of the day, when the sun   37
was rising with those stars that were with the sun

when God first created all the world. Despite my fear of that   40
beast,

I found hope, both in this new morning and the rising of   43
those stars. But this hope was not so great that I did not fear when
I saw a lion.

He appeared as if he were approaching me with great hunger,   46
and it seemed that he lifted his head up proudly, trying to scare
the air itself.

And not far from him I saw a wolf coming toward me, hungry   49
and starved beyond all belief. How many people she has brought
great grief!

She scared and depressed me with the sight of her desperation   52
so greatly that I then gave up all hope of reaching the top of the
mountain.

And just like someone who is very much pleased in wealth,   55
but weeps and angers when his money is lost, I went back.

Still that wolf followed, pushing me farther back into that   58
wood where the sun does not shine.

61   And as I fell back into the destruction of that wood, a figure appeared before me, looking like one who had little voice for lack of speaking in a long time.

64   At the sight of him in that lonely place I cried out, "Have mercy on me, whatever you are, whether a spirit or a living man!"

67   It replied, "I am not a man, although I was. My family was from Lombard, and my parents from Mantua.

70   I was born late in the rule of Julius Caesar, and grew up in Rome while Augustus ruled, in the age of the lying gods.

73   I was a poet and sang of the son of Anchises, who traveled to Rome after Troy was burned down.

76   But as for you, why do you return to this place rather than climb the Mount of Joy which leads to the place where all men are happy?"

79   "Are you Virgil, the writer of great words?" My voice trembled as I spoke:

82   "Great honor and light to all poets! I hope now that all my joy and dedication in studying your works serve me well!

85   You are my master, and you are the creator of the style with which I write and by which I have received much praise.

88   Look, eternal master, at the creature from which I flee. For the sake of my soul, I beg you to protect me from her, for she has frightened me to death."

91   He answered, seeing my fear, "If any man hopes to escape this place, he must take another path,

94   for that creature which stands before you will let no one pass.

She will track down and kill anyone, but is never satisfied,   97
for in eating her prey she grows ever hungrier.

She will mate with any creature, and will surely mate with   100
many more until the Greyhound comes to slaughter her.

This Greyhound will not feed on men's possessions, but   103
rather on virtue, love, and understanding. He will come from a
land between Feltro and Feltro,

and it will be through him that a new life is brought to Italy,   106
for which the men Nisus, Turnus, and Euryalus, and the maid
Camilla died.

He shall drive her through every city until she returns to   109
Hell, from which envy sent her to the world in the first place.

For this reason I think it best for you to follow me; I will   112
guide you through the eternal world,

where you will hear desperate wailing and see old souls   115
destroyed as they cry over the pain of the second death.

Then you will see men in fire, and yet pleased to be in it, for   118
they know that they will one day rise above to join the choir of
Heaven.

But if you wish to see Heaven itself, a worthier soul will have   121
to take you there, and I will leave you with her,

for the King has forbidden me to enter Heaven, because I   124
rebelled against him while I was living.

He has authority over all the lands and the seas and the air,   127
and in them he has his throne and his city; how happy are the
people he chooses to live in that city!"

130   And I responded, "Poet, by the power of this God that you did not know in life, lead me, so that I may escape the woe of this place.

133   Lead me to Peter's gate and guide me to see the sad spirits of Hell."

136   He then began to walk, and I followed him.

Canto I Notes

The narrator, Dante, awakes in a dark wood. As he walks through it, he finds a mountain at the edge of the woods, with the sun's light streaming over it. After resting shortly, he travels up the mountain to reach the top, but is stopped by a panther, which blocks his way, and he nearly turns back several times. He notices that it is morning, which gives him some hope, but then he spots a hungry lion, and a starving wolf. Dante gives up the hope of reaching the top of the mountain, and retreats back towards the wood. As he does, he sees a figure in the distance: It is the spirit of Virgil, the great Roman poet, who assures him the wolf will be defeated. Virgil asks Dante to follow him up the mountain, explaining that he will show him Hell and Purgatory, and another spirit will show him Heaven. They depart on the path to Hell.

1. journey of our life: This phrase is taken to mean exactly halfway through the life of a man, which is taken to be 70 years according to Psalm 90.10. Therefore, the events of the Inferno take place when Dante is 35.

33. panther: The panther is taken to symbolize sins of fraud or deceit, which will appear later in the *Inferno.* The word for 'panther' is sometimes translated as 'leopard.'

38-40. those stars...the world: According to popular tradition at the time, the sun was positioned in the constellation Aries during the creation. This indicates that the story takes place around the spring equinox. The exact time period of the story will be indicated by later events.

45. *lion:* The lion is taken to symbolize sins of violence.

49. *wolf:* The wolf is taken to symbolize sins of immoderate or unnatural desire, also called incontinence, which include such sins as gluttony, anger, and lust.

62-72. *a figure:* The figure is Virgil, the great poet; he symbolizes human reason in the work. The meaning of the passages concerning his looking as though he had not spoken for awhile, and the period during which he lived is somewhat disputed; however, we know that he was born in 90 B.C. near Mantua, a city in Lombardy, which is a northern Italian region, and died in 19 B.C.

73. *son of Anchises:* Aeneas, a figure from mythological history. The *Aeneid* is the story of his journeys, which end in the founding of Rome.

101. *the Greyhound...Feltro and Feltro:* This is a very obscure phrase, and there are multiple possible interpretations. The Greyhound is likely to be either Christ (in his second coming) or Can Grande della Scala, a leader of the Ghibellines; but the latter interpretation is more often accepted. Feltro and Feltro could refer to the geographical region between Feltre and Montefeltro; or if read as 'felt and felt,' it could refer to humble origins. There are many interpretations, and much dispute as to Dante's intended meaning.

107-108. *Nisus, Turnus...Euryalus...Camilla:* These four all died during the war that is documented in the end of the Aeneid. Their apparent significance here is that they all died for Italy.

117. *second death:* Damnation to Hell, which is the death of the spirit following the death of the body.

118. *men in fire:* Those in Purgatory, who are in a fire of cleansing.

121. worthier soul: Beatrice. She will be discussed further in Canto 2, but she does not make an actual appearance in the *Inferno.*

133. Peter's gate: Although in modern times Peter's gate refers to the entrance to Heaven, here it refers to the entrance to Purgatory.

Canto II

1   The sun was now setting and the light dimming. The darkening air was sending all the creatures of the earth to sleep, but I

4   was just preparing myself to face a war, not only of the journey itself, but also of the woe I would find. I will here record what happened from my memory, which makes no mistake.

7   Muses! O you great geniuses! Aid me! Memory, you have given me the words to write, here all will see your true nobility.

10   I said to him, "Poet, my guide, before you allow me to travel this terrible path, look at me and tell me if I am strong enough for it.

13   It was you who said that the father of Silvius went into the immortal world with his mortal body, even though he was corruptible.

16   So if the enemy of all evil allowed him this great pleasure, even while knowing all the things that would come from him, and what he was,

19   that cannot surprise intelligent men, because he was chosen to lead Rome, and the Empire as well by God's very design.

22   Both of these, it could be said, were decided and willed by God to be the throne of the successor of the great Peter.

On this journey, he learned of things that brought him and   25
the papal mantle great victory.

Later, the chosen messenger of God's words came there and   28
gave assurance that faith in God is the true faith to lead men to
Heaven.

But, why should I see the eternal world? I am not Aeneas,   31
and I am not Paul. Others would not consider me worthy; I do
not even consider myself worthy!

So if I do go on this journey, I worry that I will not be able to   34
understand or appreciate fully what I am being shown. But you
are wise, and you know better that I."

And now I became like a person who makes up his mind to   37
do one thing, and then decides to do another, and gives up what
he started,

because on that dark hill I quickly decided not to continue   40
what I had begun.

"If I understand you correctly," that magnificent spirit said,   43
"you have become a coward in your soul;

this happens to many men frequently, and forces them away   46
from their noble attempts, just like poor eyesight frightens an
animal in the dark.

I will try to help your fear by telling you about why I came   49
here and what I was told that first caused me to have pity for you.

I was one of the souls that lived in Limbo, and a lady came   52
to me, so beautiful and lovely that I begged her to allow me to
serve her.

Her eyes were greater than the stars, and she spoke to me   55
with the voice of an angel. She said to me,

58   'You kind spirit from Mantua, you who are still well known in the world of the living, and will be remembered until the end of time,

61   a friend of mine who has been hurt by bad fortune has wandered from the straight path on a lonely hillside and has been greatly frightened.

64   There is news in heaven that he is already lost; I fear it is too late for me to save him.

67   But go to him, and use your persuasive words and anything else necessary to make sure he returns to the straight path, so that I may no longer worry about him.

70   My name is Beatrice; I came from heaven, and I desire to return there soon, but it was love that made me come to you, and it is love that makes me speak.

73   When again I stand before God, I will make sure I mention your name to him many times.' After this, Beatrice said nothing. I replied,

76   'Lady, you have great virtue; it is the only thing that causes men to rise above lies and into heaven,

79   your command is so good to me that even if I completed it this instant it would not be soon enough. All you must do is tell me what you want, and I will do it.

82   But if I may ask you, how is it that you came into this dreadful place when you could have stayed in a place of joy?'

85   'Since you are so curious to know, I will tell you now,' she replied, 'how I came to this place without fear.

88   We should only fear those things that can harm us; those things that have no power shouldn't be feared.

God, being gracious, has allowed me to come into this place   91
without feeling the misery here or the heat of the flames.

In Heaven there is a lady who weeps so much for the man   94
to whom I send you, that God has lifted the ban on entering Hell
from heaven.

It was this lady that called to Lucia and said, "Dante, who is   97
faithful to you, is in great need. I ask you to take care of him."

Lucia, the enemy of all evil, came to me while I was sitting   100
next to the honorable Rachel.

She said to me, "Beatrice, the delight of God himself, why is   103
it that you haven't helped that man that loves you so much that
he separated himself from common people for your sake?

Haven't you heard him crying? Haven't you seen that he   106
is near death as he struggles with that river that is even more
fearsome than the ocean?"

And there was never anyone who moved so quickly to help   109
themselves or run from a threat than I was after Lucia told me

to come down here, for I thought that your good words,   112
which honor you and those who have read your works, would
serve you well.'

After she had said all these things, she turned her eyes away,   115
full of tears; this only prompted me to move more quickly.

So I have come to you, just as she asked, and I have saved   118
you from the beast that was blocking the shortest way up the
mountain.

So, what is your problem? Why, why must you hesitate?   121
Why are you being such a coward?

124   Why, even when three women in heaven have shown their concern, and I have given my oath to show you something great, are you not bold?"

127   Just like petals that droop and close at night, and then open again in the morning,

130   so I did the same with my strength, though I was exhausted; a great hope rushing back into me, I said to him like someone who has just been set free,

133   "Thanks be to her who has helped me in her compassion! And thanks to you, for listening to her and coming to me so swiftly!

136   With your words you have set me back in the desire to journey, and to do what I first set out to do.

139   Now we can go, for we have the same goal; you are my guide and my master." These were the things I said to him. When he turned to leave,

142   I followed him in the steep and savage path.

CANTO II NOTES

Dante begins by invoking the Muses as well as his memory to record factually the events that he has experienced. He continues his conversation with Virgil, and questions whether he is worthy of a journey of epic proportions into Hell, while Aeneas and Paul were granted that journey. Dante becomes terrified, so Virgil explains the story of his coming to Dante: Beatrice came down from Heaven at the prompting of Mary to talk to Dante and convince him to turn from his life of sin. Virgil then went out from Hell to meet Dante. Back in the narrative, Virgil's story reaffirms Dante's strength and courage, and the two set out.

7. Muses: The Muses were the goddesses of ancient mythology who inspired creativity in literature and the arts. An invocation of the Muses is typical in this sort of work.

13. father of Silvius: Aeneas.

19-20. he was chosen to lead Rome: Dante believed that the Romans and the Holy Roman Empire were both established directly by God. Aeneas, therefore, was chosen to establish Rome, the location of the papacy, the Pope being the successor to Peter under the tradition that the Apostle Peter was the original Pope.

28. chosen messenger: The Apostle Paul.

52. Limbo: The location in Hell where the unbaptized reside. We will see it in detail in Canto 4.

52. a lady: Beatrice, who is named in line 70.

61. a friend of mine: Dante.

70. Beatrice: Beatrice was a woman whom Dante loved from the time they were both children. She, however, married another man, and died while still young; she greatly influenced Dante.

94. In heaven...a lady: Mary, the mother of Jesus.

97. Lucia: A saint; she was the patroness of vision. It is not clear why Dante mentions her. She also appears in *Purgatorio* and *Paradiso*.

102. Rachel: The wife for whom Jacob worked a total of fourteen years to marry.

C ANTO III

1   THROUGH ME IS THE WAY INTO THE DREADFUL CITY.
THROUGH ME IS THE WAY TO AN ETERNAL SUFFERING.
THROUGH ME IS THE WAY TO A LOST PEOPLE.

4   JUSTICE PROMPTED MY DIVINE CREATOR;
HE IS THE DIVINE AND HIGHEST POWER,
THE GREATEST KNOWLEDGE AND THE FIRST LOVE.

7   ONLY THE ETERNAL THINGS WERE MADE BEFORE
I WAS, AND I EXIST FOR ALL ETERNITY.
ABANDON ALL HOPE, YOU WHO ENTER IN!

10   These were the words I found written at the top of a gate. I said, "Master, I cannot quite understand what these words mean."

13   And he, being knowledgeable, said to me, "Here you must abandon all hesitation, and you must put out all cowardice.

16   We have reached the place of which I told you; here you will see only miserable people, those who have given up their intellect."

19   He put his hand on me to comfort me, and with a helpful smile he led me among the hidden things.

22   Hearing the cries and loud complaints echoing through that dark air, I wept as soon as we had set out.

Strange phrases, evil curses, angry speech, words of pain,   25
screeching voices, and the sound of hands beating chests

all rose and swirled about in that air, and will do so through   28
all time just like sand that is swept up by a strong whirlwind.

And I said to him in terror, "Dear spirit, what are these   31
sounds I hear? Who are these people so gripped with fear?"

And he said to me, "This miserable place holds the people   34
that were neither evil nor good in life.

See, they are mixed with the angels that were neither   37
rebellious towards God nor stood with God, but stood only for
themselves.

In order that Heaven might remain perfect, they were cast   40
out; but now Hell will not receive them either, for that would
bring some glory for the punished."

I said, "Master, what is the reason they cry so hard?" He   43
replied, "I will tell you briefly:

These spirits no longer have even the hope of dying, and   46
their blind lives have brought them so low that they wish they
could have any other fate.

The living world will let them have no fame; they are rejected   49
by both Mercy and Justice. Let us not talk more about them; look
at them, and let us continue."

When I looked again, I saw a large banner that flew around   52
in a circle so quickly it seemed as though it would never stop.

Behind it was a line of people so long I could not believe how   55
many souls death had claimed!

After I identified a few of them, I saw the spirit of that man   58
who, being a coward, made the great refusal.

61   Seeing him I understood that this group was certainly the group of all cowards, hated by both God and the enemies of God.

64   These cursed people, who never truly lived, were naked and were being stung constantly by horseflies and wasps that surrounded them.

67   The insects drew blood from their faces, which mixed with their tears and fell to the ground, where repulsive worms feasted on it.

70   Looking just past them, I saw men gathering at the bank of a large river, and asked, "Master, tell me,

73   who are these people, and why are they so eager to cross the river, as I see them in this dark light?"

76   And he said, "You will know what is happening with them once we reach the shore of this river, called the Acheron."

79   With this I feared that I had offended him and I walked with my eyes down, and did not speak a word until we came to that river.

82   Now coming toward the shore in a boat was an old man with white hair, yelling, "Woe be to you, you sinful souls!

85   Forget all your hopes of Heaven, for I am here to take you to the other shore of eternal dark, of fire and ice.

88   And you there, you living man, stay away from those who are dead!" But when he saw that I had no intention of moving,

91   he said, "You must travel another way to get across to the other shore. A lighter boat is needed to carry you."

94   But my guide said, "Charon, don't work yourself up. Our trip in your boat has been decided in Heaven, where everything that is decided must happen. Do not question it any longer."

Now silence came upon the hairy cheeks of Charon, who is   97
the boatman of that river, who has circles of fire around his eyes.

But while this was happening, those souls, tired and naked,   100
had become pale, and they gnashed their teeth at Charon's harsh
words.

There they cursed God and their parents and all mankind,   103
and the place and time of their conception and birth.

But nonetheless they all wept aloud as they gathered together   106
at the shore that waits for all men who have no fear for God,

that place where the demon Charon, with eyes like burning   109
coals, signals them and leads them away, and hits with his oar all
who try to delay.

Just like how in the autumn leaves fall to the ground one by   112
one until not a single one is left on the tree,

so the evil children of mankind left the shore one by one   115
as each was called for, just like a bird will return to his handler
when called upon.

So those souls travel across the dark water, and indeed, even   118
before they reach the other shore, there are more waiting on that
bank.

"My son," the good master said, "all people who die under   121
God's punishment gather here from every country; and they
desire to go across, for they are compelled to do so by Justice.

A good soul never comes this way; that is the reason Charon   124
complained about you; now you surely understand what he said."

After he said this, a terrifying earthquake overtook that   127
entire place so horridly that I sweat just in recalling it.

130   A whirlwind rose up out of the dry ground, giving off a
blinding red light, and the wind shocked all my senses,

133   and like a man taken by sleep, I fainted.

CANTO III NOTES

Dante reads the warning written on the gate at the entrance of Hell, and they enter through. Hearing great weeping, Dante immediately breaks into tears himself. Questioning Virgil, he finds that the weeping is the sounds of the opportunists, or the lukewarm: those that did no evil on earth, but did no good either. They are within the gate of Hell, but they are not truly in Hell. They chase after a banner, and their blood and tears fall to the ground and are eaten by worms. Virgil sees the bank of a great river, the Acheron. Coming across is Charon, the ferryman of the dead, preparing to bring spirits across. Seeing Dante, he warns him that he must go into Hell some other way, but Virgil insists. Spirits are collecting at the bank, waiting to be carried away. Virgil explains why they are there, and then Dante faints in fear.

17-18. those who...their intellect: That is to say, sinning is a deliberate choice.

34-69. THE OPPORTUNISTS: The first group Dante meets are the opportunists, also called the lukewarm or neutrals. They are all those who committed no particular sin, but did not stand for God or goodness. This group includes the angels who sided with neither God nor Satan. Their punishment is painful stings from insects. In addition, they are not only rejected by God, for they were not faithful to him, but they are also, in a sense, rejected by those in Hell, for they did no evil.

37-39. the angels: It is important to note that the idea of angels who chose no side in the rebellion in Heaven was more traditional (at the time) than biblical. Also, this is the only instance in Hell of angels and humans mixing: Those who sided with Satan guard another gate (they appear in Canto 8), and Satan himself is in the deepest circle (he appears in Canto 34).

50. Mercy and Justice: In explaining the fate of the opportunists, Virgil introduces the two forces of Heaven and Hell: Grace governs in Heaven, and justice in Hell.

59-60. that man...great refusal: It is not certain who Dante describes here (and from early commentaries, it appears that readers at the time of the writing did not know to whom Dante was referring either), but there are a few possibilities. The man is most likely Pope Celestine V, who in 1294 resigned from the papacy, causing Boniface VIII to become Pope. Dante viewed Boniface VIII as evil (he appears in Canto 19), and therefore may have viewed Celestine V as being guilty for Boniface VIII becoming Pope. Alternatively, Dante may be referring to Pontius Pilate, who refused to pass judgment on Jesus.

78. the Acheron: The Acheron is the river in Greek mythology over which the dead are transported by Charon. It serves the same purpose here.

87. fire and ice: Dante departs from the traditional biblical view of Hell as a 'lake of eternal fire' and makes heat and fire punishments for only some sins. In addition, the center of Hell is a frozen lake.

97. Charon: In Greek mythology, Charon was the ferryman of the underworld: He carried those who had died across the Acheron and Styx.

123. they desire...by Justice: Dante argues here and at other times that because God's judgment is perfect according to Justice, those who are condemned understand their sin once they are in Hell, and as a result are compelled to desire punishment.

Canto IV

1   My deep sleep was abruptly ended by a loud thunderclap; I woke up like one who is aroused by force.

4   I stood up and looked around with my eyes now rested, so that I could determine where I was.

7   Truly, I found myself at the edge of a large abyss, the sad valley filled with loud eternal wailing.

10   That valley is so filled with fog, and deep and dark, that I could not see anything it contained, though I looked carefully.

13   "Let us go down into the unseen world now," the poet, who had become pale, started. "I will go first, and you will follow."

16   But I, seeing how frightened he was, said, "How can I go there if you are frightened, and you are the one who has calmed my fear?"

19   And he said, "The great pain of these people who live below have given my face a color of pity, which you mistake for fear.

22   Let us go down now; the path is long." So he went forward, and I followed into the first circle that runs around the abyss.

25   As I heard it, the only cry from that place were the sighs that made the air tremble.

The sighs came out of a great many infants, women, and   28
men, though from sadness and not torture.

The kind master asked me, "Why do you not ask who these   31
are before you? I will have you know, before we continue,

that they had no sin; they did good works, but this was not   34
enough, for they did not have baptism, which is the gateway into
the faith that you have.

And, if they lived in a time before Christianity, then they   37
did not worship God in the way they should have. I am such a
person.

It is for this flaw, and not another evil, that we are lost and   40
are punished by having no hope, and only eternal longing."

My heart was greatly saddened in hearing him, for I saw   43
some good men among the souls in Limbo.

"Tell me, master and lord," I began, for I wanted to be sure of   46
the faith that rights all wrongs,

"has there ever been a soul that has gone from this place   49
to Heaven by his own works, or by the works of another?" He,
understanding my insufficient speech,

said, "When I was new to this place, I saw a great lord enter   52
here; he wore a crown as a sign of his triumph.

He came and took away the soul of the first father, Adam,   55
and his son, Abel, and Noah, and Moses, God's faithful lawmaker,

and Abraham, David the King, Israel, as well as his father and   58
sons, Rachel, for whom he worked for many years to win,

and many others, and he blessed them. But I should tell you   61
that before that, no human soul was ever saved from this place."

64   We had not stopped while he was talking, but had continued on the path, and while doing so, passed a group of souls gathered like trees in a deep wood.

67   And we had not gone far away from where I had been sleeping when I saw a light that broke open the dark.

70   We were still a short way away from that place, but we were not so far that I could not make out some of the honorable men that were there.

73   "O you who hold command of all art and science, tell me, who are these men, and what honor do they have that separates them from all the others?"

76   And he said, "Their honor, which is known in your lifetime, goes up to Heaven and gains Heaven's grace; this sets them apart."

79   Meanwhile I heard a voice, saying, "All honor to the great poet! Though his soul left us, it now returns!"

82   After the voice was silent, I saw four giants approaching, who seemed neither sad nor happy.

85   My master began, "Look at the one with the sword in hand, see how he leads the others.

88   That man is Homer, the master of poetry. The one behind him is Horace, the satirist. The third is Ovid, and the fourth, Lucan.

91   Because all of them share with me in the call you just heard, they honor me, and honor me well."

94   And so I saw that great group led by the master of all song, who soars like an eagle above all other poets.

97   When they had talked awhile, they turned and greeted me, and seeing this, my master smiled.

And they gave me much more honor by inviting me to join   100
them; and so I became the sixth in that group of intellectuals.

As we moved toward the light, we talked about many things   103
that I do not record, but were good to be spoken then.

We reached a great castle, circled by seven walls and guarded   106
by a good stream.

We passed over it as though it was dry ground, and entering   109
through seven gates with them I came upon a blooming meadow.

The people there had slow and solemn eyes, and they had   112
great authority in their stance. They spoke infrequently, with
soft voices.

So we went off to one side where it was very open and filled   115
with light, and we could see all those assembled there.

Standing there in front of me were great spirits, and I still   118
feel greatly exalted having the privilege of seeing them.

I saw Electra there with many others, Hector and Aeneas   121
among them, and Caesar with his armor and his hawk-like eyes.

I saw Camilla and Penthesilea on the other side, and King   124
Latinus sitting with his daughter Lavinia.

I saw Brutus (the one who drove away Tarquin), and Lucretia,   127
Julia, Marcia, and Cornelia, and Saladin standing by himself.

And looking a little higher up, I saw the master of the wise,   130
and many philosophers with him.

All there look at him and all honor him. I saw Socrates and   133
Plato closest to him,

136   and Democritus, who claimed all things happen through chance, and Diogenes, Anaxagoras, Thales, Zeno, Empedocles, and Heraclitus.

139   I saw the collector of medicines (I mean Dioscorides), and Orpheus, Tully, Linus, the moral Seneca,

142   Euclid the geometer, Ptolemy, Hippocrates, Avicenna and Galen, and Averroës, who wrote the Great Commentary.

145   I cannot list all those I saw here, because this long work forces me to continue, so sometimes my words do not fully describe what I saw.

148   So our group of six divided into two groups, and my intelligent guide led me in a different direction, away from the peaceful quiet into the trembling air.

151   So I came to a place where there is no source of light.

CANTO IV NOTES

Dante is awoken on the other side of the Acheron by a loud noise, and looks around to find a gaping chasm before him, filled with clouds and the sounds of weeping. Where Dante and Virgil are standing, however, there is only the sounds of sighs. Virgil explains that they are in the first circle of Hell, Limbo, where the unbaptized reside. Dante asks whether a spirit can ever leave Limbo by doing good, but Virgil explains that the only spirits that left Limbo were those whom Jesus took with him when he descended into Hell to announce his victory. Moving along, Dante sees a group of individuals set apart from the rest; they are the five great poets in Hell, the group that includes Virgil. They welcome Dante, and then proceed to a great castle, where they find many great poets, heroes, philosophers, scientists, mathematicians, and the like. After observing some of them, the two poets go on, and return to the darkness.

7. large abyss: Hell is conical in shape; the other bank of the Acheron is next to the first cliff they must descend.

20. pity: Virgil will later scold Dante for having pity on the souls in Hell. This may seem strange on account of Virgil showing pity here, but in reality, the pity Virgil has is only for those who are in Limbo, who did no wrong.

23-150. THE UNBAPTIZED: The first of the nine circles of Hell is Limbo, where the unbaptized reside. They are the collection of both those who lived before Christ was on earth and did not worship God in the proper manner, and those who lived while the Christian church existed, but either ignored or rejected it. They are those who had no baptism, but were guilty of no sin. Dante goes against the religious tradition in including unbaptized adults.

52. a great lord: Jesus, who entered into Hell after dying on the cross. His entry into Hell is further discussed later.

62-63. before that...this place: In Dante's construction of Christianity, the only means to Heaven is through faith; works alone are not enough.

82. four giants: Not literally giants, but rather, giants in terms of their accomplishments.

88. Homer: The great Greek poet; his best-known works are the *Odyssey* and the *Iliad.*

89-90. Horace...Ovid...Lucan: The three great Latin poets, Virgil being the fourth. Horace was known to Dante as the author of *Ars poetica,* the Art of Poetry; Ovid was the author of *Metamorphoses,* a work detailing mythology; and Lucan was the author of *Pharsalia,* which detailed the civil war between Pompey and Julius Caesar.

101. the sixth: When Dante meets the poet Statius in Purgatory, then Dante becomes the seventh, completing the number of great poets.

106. seven walls: The seven-walled castle is the home of the greatest unbaptized historical figures. The seven walls are taken to symbolize the seven virtues.

121-123. Electra there...and Caesar: Electra was the mother of Dardanus, who helped found Troy; Hector and Aeneas were Trojans, and Caesar was (supposedly) descended from Aeneas.

124-126. Camilla...Lavinia: All are characters of the *Aeneid.*

127-129. Brutus...Saladin: All are Romans, except Saladin, who was an Egyptian sultan who drove out the Crusaders.

130-131. master of the wise: Aristotle, who was considered the greatest of all the philosophers.

133-138. Socrates...Heraclitus: All are Greek philosophers.

139-141. Dioscorides...Seneca: Dioscorides was an early authority on plant medicines; all the others are poets.

142-144. Euclid...Commentary: Euclid was a mathematician, Ptolemy was primarily an astronomer, Hippocrates was a physician, and Galen a medicine man. Avicenna was a Muslim medicine man, and Averroës was a Muslim commentator on the works of Aristotle. The Great Commentary is his commentary on Aristotle's *De anima,* 'On the Soul.'

C A N T O   V

1   So I descended from the first circle to the second, which is smaller but offers much greater pain, which causes weeping.

4   There the terrible Minos stands gnashing his teeth. He examines the sins of those entering that place, and judges them and gives them a place in Hell by wrapping his tail around his body.

7   By this I mean that evil souls come before him and confess everything, and he, being an expert in sin,

10   knows to which place that soul should be sent; the number of times Minos wraps his tail around himself is the level to which the sinner is sent.

13   There is constantly a crowd before him; every soul takes its turn before judgment. They speak their sins and hear his decree, and are thrown down.

16   As soon as Minos saw me, he stopped and said, "You who have come to this place of suffering,

19   be careful where you go and whom you trust; wide is the gate…do not be deceived!" My master replied, "Why do you complain?

22   Do not attempt to block his journey, for it is willed in Heaven, where there is one who does what he wishes. Say nothing else."

Now sounds of sadness began to overcome my ears, for I was   25
in a place where great cries pounded against me.

I was in that place where all light is suppressed, and sounds   28
like the sea under a great storm, when great winds push against it.

There was a hellish hurricane, never resting, which pushed   31
spirits about violently, constantly harassing them with its force.

When sinners come up to the landslide in front of the   34
hurricane, they cry out and curse the power of God.

I learned that those people who suffer this are sent there for   37
the sin of lust, having given up their intellect to live for their
bodies.

Just like birds fly on the air in cold weather, so does that   40
hurricane hold up those punished spirits:

It pushes them up and down, to and fro. They have no hope   43
of redemption, and no hope of rest or a lesser punishment.

Just like cranes sing out a sad note flying in long lines, so did   46
those spirits I saw coming towards me on that terrible wind

cry out. So I asked, "Master, who are those souls who suffer   49
in this dark air?"

"The first one you should notice," my master responded,   52
"once was an empress over many languages.

Her sin of lust became so great that she even made laws to   55
pardon herself from the scandal she created.

Her name is Semiramis; we read that she was the wife and   58
successor of Ninus; she ruled over the land that the Sultan now
rules.

61   That next spirit killed herself for love, and betrayed Sichaeus after he had died. After her is the lustful Cleopatra.

64   See Helen, who caused much grief for many years. See the great Achilles, who fought love in his last battle.

67   See Paris and Tristan…" and he named many more spirits who died because of love.

70   Upon hearing my teacher name all these famous ancient women and men, I felt a great pity, and it greatly upset me.

73   My first words were, "Poet, I would like to speak with those two spirits who travel together and fly so lightly in the wind."

76   And he said, "You will see them as they approach, and then you may ask them to speak with you. For the sake of their love, they will come to you."

79   As soon as the wind brought them near, I yelled out, "You tormented souls, come speak with us, if God does not forbid it!"

82   Just like doves called by desire and moving by their own will fly through the air to their nest,

85   so those spirits left the place where Dido suffers and approached us through the disgusting air, for my cry was so compelling.

88   "O living man, kind and innocent, you who have come through the dark air to visit those of us whose blood has stained the earth,

91   if God were our friend, we would pray to Him to bless you for pitying our terrible punishment.

94   Whatever you wish to talk about will please us in this place where the wind is quiet.

The land where I was born is by the shore where the Po and   97
all its rivers end.

Love, which quickly fills a good heart, captured this man   100
because of the body I had, which was taken from me when I died,
and I still grieve over my death.

                                                                103

Love, which allows one who is loved no choice in whether to
return that love, took me so strongly, because of his beauty, that
still I am bound by it.

                                                                106

Love brought both of us to the same death. Surely, Caina is
waiting for him who killed us!" These were the words that came
to us.

                                                                109

When I heard them, I bent my head and looked down until
the poet asked, "What is it you are thinking?"

                                                                112

When I finally replied, I said, "How many good thoughts,
how strong a love, have brought them to this painful path!"

                                                                115

Then I said to them, "Francesca, your pain brings me to tears
of pity.

                                                                118

But I ask, in a time when you were content, how did love
cause you to realize your evil desire?"

And she said, "Oh, it is the worst pain to think back on good   121
times! Your teacher knows this to be true.

Yet if you wish to know what the beginning of our love was,   124
I will tell you, even though I weep just thinking of it.

One day, in order to pass the time, we read about Lancelot,   127
and how love took him. We were alone, and suspected nothing
to happen.

130   And yet countless times that reading caused our eyes to meet, and our faces went pale. But it was one part of the story that defeated us:

133   When we read about how a smile was kissed by its true lover, this man, who stays with me forever,

136   kissed my mouth while his whole body trembled. Galeotto was the book, and also the author; indeed, we read no more of it that day."

139   And while she said these things, the other spirit wept, and I fainted from pity, as though I had died.

142   So I fell, just like a dead body.

Canto V Notes

Dante and Virgil descend to the second circle, and find Minos, who judges sinners: They arrive before him and confess their sins, and he determines their place in Hell. Dante sees a large whirlwind that runs around the second circle, sweeping spirits with it. He finds that they are the carnal, those guilty of adultery. Virgil points out Semiramis, Dido, Cleopatra, Helen, Achilles, Paris, Tristan, and many more. Dante asks to speak to two spirits in particular (they are Francesca and Paolo). Francesca tells the story of how they fell in love, and Dante reflects on how it was love that caused their death. Francesca explains that they were killed by her husband, Gianciotto, who found her kissing Paolo one day. Dante then faints out of pity for them.

2-3. *which causes weeping:* In the first circle, Limbo, the spirits sighed; here, where there is true punishment, they weep.

4. *Minos:* He was a son of Zeus, and one of the judges of the underworld according to mythology.

25-142. *THE CARNAL:* The second circle of Hell contains the carnal, or the adulterers. In putting the carnal in the place of least punishment (apart from the unbaptized in Limbo), Dante expresses his belief that because adultery is very much like love (in fact, it is considered excessive love), it is the least bad of all the sins.

34. *the landslide:* We learn later that when Christ entered Hell, a great earthquake occurred and caused many landslides.

44-45. no hope...lesser punishment: This is the law of Hell: The punishments continue forever, and never grow less terrible.

53-54. empress over many languages: We will find she is Semiramis, who ruled over Babylon, a nation of many languages.

56. laws to pardon herself: She made incest legal, and it was believed that this was because she had committed incest with her son.

59. Ninus: It was said that he met Semiramis when she was married to one of his generals, Onnes. He took her and married her, causing Onnes to kill himself.

60. Sultan: The area that had been Ninus' kingdom was, at Dante's time, ruled over by a group of Egyptian soldiers called the Mameluke Sultanate.

61-62. next spirit...betrayed Sichaeus: The spirit is Dido, who founded Carthage. Sichaeus was her husband, and she vowed to remain faithful to him after his death. However, she fell in love with Aeneas. When Aeneas abandoned her, she killed herself.

63. Cleopatra: The queen of Egypt. She was romantically involved with Julius Caesar, Marc Antony, and two of her brothers (this was tradition in her family of royals).

64. Helen: Helen of Troy (as she came to be known), the wife of King Menelaus of Sparta. She eloped with Paris, which began the Trojan War.

65. Achilles: The great warrior of the Trojan War, who was invincible except for his heel (according to later writings). In some versions of the story, he fell in love with Polyxena, the daughter of King Priam of Troy. Priam tried to wed them believing that their marriage would end the war, but Polyxena's brothers, Paris and Deiphobus, shot Achilles in the heel with an arrow, thus killing him.

67. Paris and Tristan: As already stated, Paris was a son of Priam, and eloped with Helen. Tristan was a character in the legend of Tristan and Isolde. The story was incredibly popular in medieval times. Many variations exist, but the basic story circles around how Tristan fell in love with Isolde, who was supposed to marry Tristan's uncle, King Mark.

74. those two spirits: We will find that they are Francesca and Paolo. Francesca was to be married to Gianciotto Malatesta. However, because Gianciotto was deformed, Francesca's father had the marriage performed between Francesca and Paolo, Gianciotto's brother. She was unaware of this switch, and they fell in love. Gianciotto discovered them together, and killed them both.

97-99. the land...rivers end: Ravenna, in Italy. The Po is a major Italian river that passes by Ravenna.

107. Caina is waiting...killed us: Caina is the division of Hell in which traitors against family are punished. Again, it was Paolo's brother and Francesca's fiancé, Gianciotto, that killed them.

118-120. how did love...desire: Dante is asking how love led her to realize that she desired Paolo.

128. Lancelot, and how love took him: They were reading the scene in the story of Lancelot the Knight in which Lancelot kissed Guinevere, King Arthur's wife.

137. Galeotto: The Italian name for Galehaut, the friend of Lancelot who arranged the meeting between him and Guinevere. He is 'the book' because the legend of Lancelot focuses greatly on Galehaut, and, indeed, part of the legend was called 'The Galehaut'; it appears that Dante thought that Galehaut was the author of the legend, when in fact the author is unknown.

C A N T O   V I

1   My mind then waking again from the faintness caused by hearing the cry of those two lovers, since their sorrow had taken over me completely,

4   I saw new punishments and new punished souls all around, no matter where I moved or looked.

7   I was in the third circle, filled with a heavy, freezing, eternal, cursed rain; neither its nature nor its amount ever changes.

10   Massive hailstones, disgusting gray water, and snow fall through the dark air, and the ground stinks from that downpour.

13   Looking over the souls submerged beneath that water is a strange, vicious monster, Cerberus, who has three barking dog-like mouths.

16   His eyes are bloodshot, his beard is black and greasy, and his hands are like claws. His talons tear away the skin of the spirits.

19   The constant rain makes the spirits howl as though they were dogs themselves; in using half of their body to protect the other, they constantly writhe on the ground.

22   When Cerberus, that foul creature, spotted us, he opened his mouths to bare his teeth at us, his whole body twitching.

My guide opened his hands, picked up some dirt, and with   25
full fists he threw it right into those hungry jaws.

Just like a dog that barks when hungry will quiet as soon as   28
he gets food, working hard to eat as quickly as possible,

so the faces of Cerberus (who barks so loud the spirits wish   31
they were deaf) changed.

We were walking over the spirits on which the rain falls, our   34
feet stepping on their false appearances that seem like people.

And every single spirit was lying down on the ground, except   37
for one, who stood up when he saw us approaching.

"You who are led through Hell," he said, "remember me, if   40
you are able, for you were born before I died."

And I said, "I think maybe it is your pain that prevents me   43
from remembering you, for I think that I have never before seen
you.

But remind me, you who live in such a terrible place, where,   46
even if there are worse punishments, none are more disgusting."

And he said, "Your city, so full of envy that it overflows with   49
it, once regarded me in a better light.

The citizens there called me Ciacco. As you can see, it is for   52
the sin of gluttony that I sit in this rain.

And I am not alone, for all the souls here are punished the   55
same for this same crime." And then he was silent.

I responded, "Ciacco, I weep greatly at your suffering, which   58
hurts me much, but tell me if you know, what is the fate of

the people of that divided city? Is there even one good man   61
there? Tell me why it has suffered so much division."

64   And he replied, "After much argument, the people will come to murder. The party of the wood will push out the other with violence.

67   But after three suns, they too will fall, and the other party will rise under one who stays close to shore.

70   This party will be in power for many years, and will greatly abuse its enemies, no matter how much they weep.

73   There are two good men, but there is not a single man who listens to them. The three sins that grip all men are envy, pride, and greed."

76   With this his tear-inducing words ended, and I said, "I wish to know more; I wish you to continue:

79   Tegghiaio, Farinata, worthy men, and Arrigo, Mosca, Jacopo Rusticucci, and all the others who intended well,

82   please tell me where they are so that I may see them, for I greatly desire to know if Heaven has made them good or if Hell has destroyed them."

85   He replied, "They are among the blackest of all souls! But a different sin has brought them even lower than I; if you go low enough, you can see them there.

88   But I ask you, when you return to the good world of the living, please remind men of me. I will say no more, so do not speak to me any longer."

91   Then his face grew distorted; he stared at me, and at long last bent his head and fell down as low as those around him.

94   And my guide said, "He will not rise from the ground again until the sound of the angels' trumpets announces the Judge's coming.

Then, every one of these will return to his tomb and have his   97
flesh once more, and will hear proclaimed his punishment for all
eternity."

So we went across that disgusting mix of spirits and rain, but   100
we slowed to talk a little about things to come.

I said, "At that judgment, when the punishment for these   103
souls is proclaimed, will their punishment be worse or better? Or
will they remain the same?"

And he responded, "Do not forget your philosophy, which   106
says that when something is more perfect, it feels greater pleasure,
and greater pain.

Although these sinners will never be perfect, they will at   109
least have more of a form than they do now."

And so we took the road that circles around that place, and   112
talked about many more things that I cannot remember, and
eventually reached the slope that leads downward.

And here we saw the great enemy, Plutus.   115

CANTO VI NOTES

Dante awakes in the third circle, the circle of the gluttons. Rain and hail falls and forms a disgusting pool in the circle. The monster Cerberus looks over those punished there, constantly frightening them with his barking and clawing. Virgil quiets Cerberus by tossing dirt into his mouth, and Virgil and Dante move on. One spirit spots them and stands up, addressing them. It is Ciacco, who delivers a prophecy concerning Florence's political parties and a looming uprising. Dante finds that several men he considered worthy are in fact punished in Hell, and more severely than Ciacco. After leaving Ciacco, Virgil explains the events that will occur at the Judgment. The canto then ends with Dante and Virgil finding Plutus.

4-111. THE GLUTTONS: The third circle of Hell is reserved for the punishment of gluttons. In modern times, gluttony is commonly viewed exclusively as overeating, whereas classically gluttony included eating food that was too expensive, that had too much seasoning, or even was eaten too eagerly. The gluttons are punished by being constantly pelted with heavy rain and hailstones; the disgusting downpour is symbolic of the disgusting habits of the gluttons.

14. Cerberus: In Greek mythology, Cerberus guarded the entrance to Hades. It seems that Dante describes him as a human with dog-like features, when he is an actual dog in classical mythology.

35-36. false appearances...like people: This serves to remind the reader that the spirits have no physical body. The retrieval of the body will be discussed in part later in this canto, and also in Canto 13.

49. your city: That is, Florence.

52. Ciacco: It is uncertain whether this Ciacco was an actual person. The name means 'hog,' and could have been a nickname.

65. the party of the wood: This party is the White Guelfs, with whom Dante was allied.

67-69. after three suns...close to shore: Ciacco here prophesies that after the party of the wood (the White Guelfs) take over, the other party (the Black Guelfs) will take control after three suns (within three years) with the aid of one who stays close to shore (Boniface VIII; the phrase 'close to shore' is roughly equivalent to our 'on the fence,' indicating that at the time Boniface seemed impartial to the events in Florence). Recall that because the events of the *Inferno* take place in 1300, but the text was written many years later, Dante's characters are prophesying events that had already occurred when the *Inferno* was written.

73. two good men: Who they are is never stated.

79-80. Tegghiaio...Rusticucci: These are all Florentines from before Dante's time. All but Jacopo Rusticucci appear in Hell later.

106-111. your philosophy: Virgil is referring to Aristotle's writings, as they were the basis of philosophy at the time. The belief referenced here is that the body and soul are only perfect, or complete, when together, so the union of body and spirit at the judgment will increase the pain experienced by those in Hell. In this reference, the word 'perfect' is taken to have the meaning 'whole' or 'complete' as opposed to 'without sin' or 'holy.'

115. Plutus: Plutus guards the fourth circle, and will be addressed at the beginning of Canto 7.

Canto VII

1   "Pape Satan, Pape Satan, aleppe!" cried Plutus with his screeching voice. The kind poet, who knows everything,

4   said to calm me, "Don't concern yourself with him. He has no power to prevent us from passing down this ledge."

7   Then he turned to Plutus' bloated face again and said, "Shut up, you cursed beast! Let your vengefulness consume you!

10   This man's journey is not without purpose; it has been so decided in Heaven, where the angel Michael cast out the rebels."

13   As sails, once blown open by the wind, will fall into a mess when the mast breaks, so that terrible beast fell down.

16   And so we went down into the fourth circle, to see more of Hell, where the evil of all the universe is kept.

19   By God's Justice, who exists who has seen and written of more tortures and punishments than I have? Why does our guilt overcome us?

22   Just like the waves over Charybdis fall on each other, so did the spirits in that circle dance their dance.

25   Here I saw more souls than ever before, on both sides; they cried out as they used their chests to push heavy weights around.

There were two groups, and they traveled toward each other   28
around the circle, and after meeting, they all turned back to
travel the other way and shouted, "Why do you hoard? Why do
you waste?"

So they moved around the circle from one point to the   31
opposite, and over and over they yelled their cry of scorn,

and when they turned around, again they walked back from   34
where they came from. Feeling a great pain in my heart

I asked, "Master, tell me if all these spirits whose heads are   37
shaven who walk to our left were clergymen."

And he said, "All of these, both on the left and the right,   40
were so narrow-sighted in their mind in their first life that they
spent nothing carefully.

They yell out clearly their cry when they meet those on the   43
other side, at the points where they turn back.

Those who have no hair were clergy, and popes, and   46
cardinals, who are so good at hoarding money."

And I said, "Master, surely I would be able to recognize some   49
of these who are charged with that crime."

But he responded, "You have not thought it through! See,   52
their life in which they did not recognize proper handling of
money has made them unrecognizable now.

They will fight for all eternity; these here will rise out of their   55
graves with clenched fists and these others with shaven heads.

Bad keeping and bad giving has robbed them of the good   58
world, and has sent them to this fight eternally. What they
experience, my words cannot describe any better.

61   Now it is evident to you, son, how pointless is the struggle to fight over money, for it is in the hands of Fortune; nonetheless, men fight and war over it;

64   all the gold under the moon would never make happy a single weary soul here."

67   "Master," I asked, "tell me about this Fortune, who holds all things in her hand."

70   And he said, "O stupid mankind, how great is your ignorance! Hear me well in this:

73   He who has made the heavens and guides them with his angels is the one whose wisdom is greater than anything;

76   he has made it so that light fills all of heaven. In the same way, he has made Fortune to preside over all the wealth,

79   and to move it from nation to nation every once in a while, and man cannot prevent it.

82   So, one nation will rule as another dies, but all obey her instructions even though they are hidden like a snake in grass.

85   Any knowledge you have cannot stop her, for she sees all things to come and does what she wants with her task, as all the other angels do with theirs.

88   She makes changes quickly and often; it is necessary that she does this, and it is for this reason that the state of the world changes so frequently.

91   She is often blamed even by those who owe her their fortune in times of profit.

94   However, she is holy and hears none of this; just like all the other angels, she is happy and does what she wants.

But come, let us move to the next circle, for the stars that   97
hung in the sky as we began are now setting; we cannot stay here
much longer."

And so we passed to a shore, where there was a great waterfall   100
that spills into a ditch filled with its water.

That water was even darker than dark purple, and just like   103
the water we moved down by a hidden pathway.

When the water reaches the end of the slope, the sad stream   106
flows into a swamp, Styx.

And I, looking carefully, could see some people in the mud,   109
naked and with angry faces.

They hit each other with not only their hands, but their feet   112
and their chests and heads, and tore each other apart with their
teeth.

The kind master said, "Son, see those who have been   115
overcome by anger; and also

there are sinners under the water, and their sighs cause the   118
bubbles you see all around in this swamp.

Stuck there they say, 'We were sullen even in the good air lit   121
up by the sun; that sullenness was inside of us,

and now we are in this black mud.' This statement they have   124
to gurgle because they cannot say all the words."

And so we traveled on the dry shore around most of that   127
disgusting swamp, constantly watching the souls there who were
eating the mud.

And at last we arrived at the base of a tower.   130

Canto VII Notes

Dante and Virgil find Plutus, the guardian of the fourth circle, crying out in nonsensical language. Moving on, they find the hoarders and the wasters, the collection of those who were too greedy with their money or who spent too wastefully. The two groups travel in the circle in opposite directions, and whenever they meet they shout at each other. In the general structure of punishment in Hell, Virgil states that their failure to recognize the handling of money properly has made them all unrecognizable. Virgil progresses to tell Dante about Fortune and her power over countries and peoples. They then travel farther, to Styx, which fills the fifth circle, where the sins of wrath and accidia are punished. The wrathful constantly attack each other, and those guilty of accidia are submerged in the swamp. Finally, Dante and Virgil arrive at a tower.

1. *"Pape Satan, Pape Satan, aleppe!"*: This is one of two nonsense statements uttered in the *Inferno* (the other is by the giant Nimrod in Canto 31). The meaning of the phrase is unknown to Dante, and likewise it is unknown to the reader. There have been many different interpretations given by translators and scholars, none of which are conclusive.

1. *Plutus:* In Greek mythology, Plutus was the god of wealth. He is not to be confused with Pluto, the god of the underworld, as Pluto is associated with Satan.

16-99. *THE HOARDERS AND WASTERS:* The fourth circle is the home of the hoarders, also called the miserly or the avaricious, and the wasters, also called the prodigal or the spendthrifts. They are grouped together because both failed to handle money in an appropriate way: The hoarders were too greedy, and the wasters spent too freely. They are in the same circle and push heavy weights around. The hoarders move in one direction, and the wasters in the other, and when they meet, the two groups turn back and travel the opposite directions, only to meet again, and so through eternity.

22. *the waves over Charybdis:* Charybdis was the name of a monster in the *Aeneid* that sucked in water to form a whirlpool and spat it up again three times a day. Here Dante is comparing the collision of the two groups with the collision of waves near Charybdis.

63. *Fortune:* Classically, Fortune was viewed as a deity; she controlled the distribution of wealth. She is discussed in Virgil's upcoming statements.

76-77. *In the same way:* Dante compares the role of the angels with controlling the lights of heaven (the heavenly bodies) with the role of Fortune in controlling wealth and power on earth.

97-98. *the stars...now setting:* By some unknown power, Virgil can see the stars and determine their positions even when it is explicitly stated at several points in the *Inferno* that the sky cannot be seen in Hell. Regardless, Virgil uses the stars to determine the time.

100-129. *THE WRATHFUL AND 'ACCIDIA':* The wrathful and those who were guilty of accidia are punished here in Styx. The wrathful, those who were excessively angry in life, constantly attack those around them. The second group of sinners are submerged in the swamp; their sin is 'accidia,' an Italian word for which the translation may either be 'sloth' or 'sullenness.' If these sinners are the slothful, then they are those guilty of laziness. If they are the sullen, then they are those who lived life in sadness and self-pity when they ought to have rejoiced in God. There are good arguments for both interpretations.

C ANTO VIII

1   I say now, that long before we reached the base of the tower, the two of us looked up at its peak,

4   for there were two flames that flickered, and another, scarcely visible flame off in the distance that seemed to answer the signal of the two.

7   I said to that sea of all knowledge, "What is this? What does the other flame reply? Who lit it?"

10   And he said, "You can already see above the dirty water what waits for us, if the fog is not too dense."

13   And I saw coming toward me a boat with a man standing in it,

16   that flew through the water faster than any arrow through air. I heard the boatman yell, "Now I have caught you, evil soul!"

19   "Phlegyas, Phlegyas, your shout has no purpose now," my master said to him, "for we are under your power for no longer than the time it takes for you to carry us across the water."

22   And just like one who becomes angry when he learns he was deceived, so Phlegyas was when he had to contain his rage.

My guide led me into the boat, and he had me follow when   25
he was in, and I noticed that the boat seemed to be holding no
weight until I entered.

But as soon as I had finished entering, the boat sped on, much   28
deeper in the water than when it holds other souls.

And while we were crossing that river, a sinner, covered in   31
mud, appeared before me and said, "Who are you, who are here
before your time?"

And I said, "Yes, I am here, but only for a time. And who are   34
you, who have become so hideous?""I am one who weeps, this
you can see!" was all he said.

"Then may you weep forever, cursed spirit! Though slime   37
covers your face, I know who you are!"

And he lashed out at me with both hands, at which my   40
master shoved him back and said, "Go back to the other dogs!"

And then he wrapped his arms around my neck and said,   43
"Blessed is the woman who bore you!

When that man was living, he was full of pride. There is not   46
a single good deed he did for him to remember, and so his spirit
is so angry down here.

How many men are up there who count themselves among   49
the kings, and yet will end up here, like pigs, their evil sins
remembered above?"

I said, "Master, I much desire to see that spirit once more   52
before we reach the other side of this river."

And he responded, "Surely, before you see the other side of   55
this river, you will find that man, for it is only right to grant such
a good wish."

58   Soon after he said this, I saw the other sinners, covered in mud, dismembering him, and I still thank God for it!

61   Every one of them was shouting "Have at Filippo Argenti!" Hearing this, that Florentine, in rage, began to bite at himself.

64   And that is where we left him; I will say no more. But I heard so great a crying that I leaned forward to better hear and see.

67   The good master said, "My son, the city called Dis is approaching, with its damned inhabitants and its great walls."

70   I replied, "Master, already I can see the mosques shining down below, glowing red like they just came out of a fire."

73   And he said, "The eternal flame makes them seem red, as you noticed, in Lower Hell."

76   So the lake led us to the moats around that place; the ramparts seemed to be made of iron.

79   Not long after, we reached a point where the shrill Phlegyas yelled, "Get out; the entrance is here!"

82   Standing around the gate I saw a thousand of those who fell from Heaven. They were shouting, "Who is this man who can travel through the land of the dead

85   while still alive?" And my all-knowing master indicated that he wished to speak to them privately.

88   Then he calmed them slightly and they said to him, "You can come with us, but let him stay, for he was foolish to enter this place.

91   Let him go back to his crazy path, if he is able, because you have led him and now you will stay here."

Reader, consider how frightened I was at their words!   94
Returning back to the land of the living seemed impossible.

"O dear guide, more than seven times you have restored my   97
confidence and have saved me from certain harm,

do not desert me when I am so distraught! If they will not   100
let us enter, let us go back the way we came, and quickly!" I said.

My lord who was my guide said, "Do not be afraid...there is   103
no one that can stop our journey, for the great one has granted it.

But wait here for me, and lift your hope, for I will not   106
abandon you here in this low place."

So he went a little farther to talk to the angels; the good   109
father left me there to wait, and peace and fear were fighting
each other in my mind.

I was not able to hear what he was saying to them, but it was   112
not before long that they all ran quickly back into the city.

And they, our enemies, quickly slammed the gates in my   115
master's face, leaving him outside. And he slowly walked back
to me.

He looked at the ground, and apparently defeated, he sighed,   118
"See who has kept me out of this place of sorrow!"

But then he said, "Even though I am confused at their actions,   121
there is no reason to worry; we will still succeed against those
inside who intend on blocking our path.

This stubbornness is their tendency...they were the same   124
way once before when they tried to block a less secret gate, and
still that gate has no bolts.

127   That gate is the one on which you read the inscription,
        and already through that gate and down to this place is coming
        without guide

130   one who will open the city for us."

Canto VIII Notes

Dante and Virgil arrive at the foot of the tower and see two lights, which appear to be signaling a distant tower. The boatman Phlegyas arrives to ferry the two across the Styx. However, as they cross, Filippo Argenti, a Florentine, rises from the mud and tries to pull Dante in. Virgil repels him, and Dante curses Argenti, causing Virgil to greatly praise Dante. Dante and Virgil eventually arrive at the gates of Dis, which is Lower Hell. It is guarded by the fallen angels, who rebelled against God. Virgil tries to obtain entry through the gate, but the angels lock them out. However, Virgil assures Dante that someone is coming who will open the gate.

19. Phlegyas: Phlegyas was a king in Greek mythology who offended the gods by burning down the temple at Delphi. Here, he is made the ferryman of souls over Styx.

27. holding no weight until I entered: Indicating once again that spirits have no weight or physical presence, whereas Dante, since he has his body, does.

61-62. Filippo Argenti: The sinner's name is revealed here. Little is known about him besides the fact that he is a Florentine, and that he had his horse shod with silver (hence 'Argenti,' which comes from the Italian word *argentare,* 'to cover with silver').

67. Dis: Dis is an alternative name for Pluto. In the *Inferno,* though, Dis is the 'city' that contains the lower divisions of Hell. It is surrounded by a great wall that is guarded by the fallen angels (and the Furies, who are mentioned in Canto 9).

70. mosques: Muslims are punished as heretics in Hell, and their places of worship are made part of the architecture.

82-83. those who fell from heaven: These are the angels who rebelled against God and were cast from Heaven.

125-126. a less secret gate: From this passage it is learned that when Christ entered Hell, the fallen angels attempted to prevent his entrance through 'a less secret gate,' which is the entrance to Hell mentioned in Canto 3.

130. one who...for us: We will find in Canto 9 that it is an angel.

CANTO IX

1   Cowardice made my face turn pale when I saw that my guide had been denied entry, and this only made him hide his own fear more quickly.

4   He stood like he was listening carefully, because he was not able to see very far in the dense fog.

7   "We must win this…if not…but one so great offered to help us…" he said, "how slow that angel is in coming to us!"

10   It was obvious to me that he was only trying to hide his first words with that last statement;

13   regardless, his words frightened me, for I took his muttering to be an indicator that the situation was worse than it actually was.

16   "Does anyone from the first circle, someone whose only punishment is the lack of hope of Heaven, ever come this far down?"

19   This I asked him. And he said, "It is very uncommon for any of us to come this way.

22   Truthfully, I have been here one time before. The witch called Erichtho, who had the power to call souls from Hell back to their bodies, once summoned me.

It was not long after I had died that she asked me to go   25
through all the rings of Hell to get a spirit back from Judecca.

That is the innermost place, and the darkest, for it is farthest   28
from heaven, which lights up everything. But don't worry…I
know the path there well.

This swamp that smells so terrible surrounds the city of   31
sadness, which now we cannot enter without angry opposition."

He said other things to me then, but I do not remember what   34
they were, for at that moment, my eyes were drawn up to the top
of the tower,

where I saw the three Furies, spattered with blood, who look   37
like women,

but have snakes around their waist, and snakes for hair,   40
which cover their foreheads.

And the poet, who knew that they were the servants of the   43
queen of all pain, said, "Look! It is the vicious Erinyes!

Megaera is on the left, Allecto is the one weeping on the   46
right, and Tisiphone is the one in the middle." And that was all
he said.

They beat their bodies with their hands and tore at the skin   49
of their breasts with sharp talons, screeching so loud that I moved
closer to the poet in fear.

"Call Medusa, that he will become stone!" they cried, looking   52
down at me, "We let Theseus go too lightly, it seems!"

"Turn the other way, and shut your eyes; if that Gorgon   55
would come and you would see her, you will be stuck here
forever,"

58 my master said, turning me around. And thinking that my hands were not enough, he used his also to cover my eyes.

61 You, intelligent reader, determine the lesson that is taught beneath the layers of these strange symbolisms.

64 But now, crossing over the waves of the disgusting swamp was a terrible noise, which made the shore tremble,

67 like how a wind caused by the clashing of cold and warm air blasts through a forest

70 and destroys trees, and brings up dust and scares animals and shepherds.

73 He took off his hands and said, "Now set your eyes on the ancient swamp where the fog is thickest."

76 And just like frogs that make waves in their pond when they see a snake coming to eat them, and all fall to the bottom like rocks,

79 so the thousand souls sank at the sight of a figure walking on Styx like it were dry land, with dry feet.

82 He waved his left hand in the fog, pushing it aside; this seemed the only task requiring any effort from him.

85 It was obvious to me that he was sent from Heaven. I turned toward my master, and he signaled me to bow before the figure.

88 How angry the figure seemed! He went up to the gate and opened it with the flick of a wand, and there was nothing to stop him.

91 "You rejects of Heaven, you despised angels!" were the first words he spoke there, "Why are you still so full of yourselves?

Why do you wish to go against the will that cannot be   94
stopped, which has increased your punishment so many times?

Why do you try to fight fate? If you remember, Cerberus had   97
the flesh of his throat and chin torn off for that same sin."

And then he turned away the way he came, and said nothing   100
to us, but looked like one whose mind is occupied by tasks more
important

than the one he is doing. And we went into the city safely,   103
having been reassured by his holy words.

We entered with no trouble, and I, eager to see what was in   106
that place,

looked around as soon as we were in. I saw in that entire   109
place crying and terrible pain.

Just like at Arles, where the Rhone flows into a marsh, and   112
at Pola, near the gulf of Quarnero, which is the border of Italy,

where the tombs make the even plain uneven, so here was   115
the plain made uneven, except these tombs were much worse,

for there were flames all around that heated the tombs red-   118
hot; there is no blacksmith that has ever made a hotter flame.

The lid of each tomb was not in place, and so the cries of the   121
hurt came from that place.

And I said, "Master, who are these souls who cry out in agony   124
as they are held in these stone chests?"

And he replied, "These are the worst of heretics, and their   127
followers, from all different false religions. The tombs are more
numerous than you can even imagine.

130   In this place, spirits are punished with those like them; some tombs are heated more and some less." Then he turned to the right,

133   and we passed between the wall and the tortures.

CANTO IX NOTES

Having been denied entry, Virgil and Dante both become frightened, though Virgil attempts to hide it. He begins to mumble to himself, which only makes Dante more frightened. Dante asks whether anyone from Limbo has ever come down as far as they. Virgil explains that while it is uncommon, he had retrieved a soul from Judecca (the innermost part of Hell) many years ago. The Furies appear, and threaten to summon Medusa. Virgil covers Dante's eyes, but just then an angel crosses over the water of Styx to the gate. With one movement of a wand, the angel opens the gate, scolds the fallen angels, and then leaves. Dante and Virgil enter through the gates and see a multitude of tombs, all made red-hot by flames.

23. *Erichtho:* Erichtho was a witch who, according to Lucan's *Pharsalia,* summoned a spirit from the underworld to prophesy the outcome of an upcoming battle. Dante here adds to that story by having Erichtho call on Virgil to retrieve that spirit.

27. *Judecca:* The innermost part of Hell, where the traitors of masters are punished.

37. *the three Furies:* The Furies were Roman deities of vengeance. In the *Aeneid,* Virgil stated the existence of three Furies, and Dante does likewise.

45. *Erinyes:* 'Erinyes' is the Greek name for the Furies, and means 'angry ones.'

52. Medusa: The Gorgon. It was said that looking at her directly would turn one into stone.

53-54. Theseus: According to tradition, Theseus was imprisoned when he entered the underworld in an attempt to rescue Proserpina, and was then rescued by Hercules. The Furies apparently wish they had killed Theseus, as it may have served as a warning for Dante and Virgil.

98-99. Cerberus: This is a reference to the story in which Hercules chained Cerberus.

112-115. Arles...Pola...tombs: Arles and Pola are both locations of large graveyards.

127. heretics: They will be discussed in detail in Canto 10.

Canto X

1   Now we went by a narrow path between the walls and those tormented, my master walking ahead of me.

4   "O great virtue, you who lead me through the circles of sin, speak to me to satisfy my curiosity if you so wish.

7   Can we see any of those who lie in these tombs? The lids are not on, and I see no guards."

10   And he said, "The tombs will be closed when the spirits return from Jehosaphat with their bodies.

13   In this area lie Epicurus and his followers: those who claimed that the soul dies with the body.

16   Soon you will know the answer to the question you asked, as well as the question you are merely thinking and have not shared with me."

19   I said, "My guide, the only reason I did not tell you what I was thinking was because you told me not to speak too much."

22   "Tuscan, you who go through the city of fire while still alive, you with such high speech, please stop here.

25   From your accent I can tell you are from the city against which I may have been too violent."

This sound had so surprised me that I trembled and moved   28
close to my guide.

But my guide said, "Turn back around! What do you think   31
you're doing? See, that is Farinata; you will see him only from the
waist up."

Our eyes already met, and his head and chest came up with   34
great hate towards Hell.

My guide quickly pushed me towards that tomb, and said,   37
"Choose your words carefully."

When I got closer, he asked me with contempt, "From what   40
family do you come?"

Because I did not wish to argue, I told him everything. He   43
lifted his eyes a little

and said, "Your family was a great enemy of mine and my   46
parents and party, and I had to drive them out twice."

"Yes, they were driven out," I replied, "but they still came   49
back from all over both times; this is a skill that your people
never learned quickly."

Then another spirit rose up from that tomb, but only to his   52
chin, so that I thought that perhaps it was on its knees.

It looked around as if hoping to see another person with me,   55
but seeing no one,

it cried, "Where is my son? Why does he not accompany you   58
if you have come here by your own intellect?"

I replied, "I am not here by my own power, but rather that   61
man over there guides me, maybe to one your son Guido hated."

64   The things he had said, as well as his punishment, was what allowed me to know who he was, and so answer his question with such precision.

67   And quickly rising he yelled, "'Hated'? What do you mean, 'hated'? Do you mean to say he is dead? His eyes no longer sparkle?"

70   And because I did not reply immediately, he fell back and did not rise again.

73   But the other spirit, who had called me over, continued his speech where he had left off as if he had not even noticed what had happened:

76   "If they were indeed so slow in learning this, then that is even greater punishment to me than this tomb.

79   But truly, the Lady who reigns here will not have her face lit fifty times before you will personally learn how hard that skill is to obtain.

82   And because you are to return to the world of the living, tell me, why are the people in that city so cruel against my family in all their decrees?"

85   To which I responded, "The great bloodshed that made the waters of Arbia red have led us to make such decrees in our assemblies."

88   He sighed, and shook his head, and replied, "In that fight I was not alone, but I did have cause to join.

91   But know that I was alone when all the men would have destroyed Florence; in fact, I said aloud that I wanted to save her."

94   "So that you may have some peace with me," I said, "please answer for me something that I find confusing.

It would appear, if I understand you correctly, that you are   97
able to see future events, but you have no knowledge of the
present."

He replied, "We are able to see, like one standing in bad   100
lighting, only things that are far away, for the King of all things
still allows us that.

But events that are about to happen, or are happening, we   103
cannot know; if others do not tell us, we have no knowledge of
mankind's current actions.

So now you surely know that we will know nothing when   106
that foresight is taken from us."

Then, as though feeling guilty for not saying so earlier, I said,   109
"Please tell that fallen man that his son still lives,

and that the only reason I did not answer was because I was   112
thinking about the question that you just answered."

But then my master was calling for me, so I quickly asked   115
that spirit to tell me the names of the others that were in that
tomb.

He said, "More than a thousand are here, including Frederick   118
II and the Cardinal. I will mention no one else."

Then he hid himself, and thinking about his fearsome words,   121
I returned to the old poet.

We began walking and he asked, "What is it that worries   124
you?" To satisfy him, I explained what that spirit had said to me.

Then that wise poet said, "Do not forget the words spoken   127
here. Now listen carefully:

130   When you stand before the great beauty of the good Lady who sees all things, you will hear from her all the events of your life."

133   Then he turned to the left, and moved toward the middle of that place, away from the wall on a path that leads into the pit

136   whose stench disgusted us already.

CANTO X NOTES

Dante and Virgil are now in Dis, in the sixth circle, where the heretics are punished in tombs. Virgil explains that at the Judgment, the spirits kept in the tombs will retrieve their bodies, and the tombs will be closed for eternity. They find Farinata, who speaks of past wars and makes a prophecy. While this is happening, though, a spirit rises and questions Dante about his son, Guido. Thinking Guido is dead, the spirit retreats back into the tomb. Farinata finishes his prophecy, and Dante learns that the spirits in Hell can see the future, but do not know the present. Dante instructs Farinata to tell the other spirit that Guido is not dead, and then Farinata states that many others are entombed with him.

1-132. THE HERETICS: The heretics are punished in the sixth circle. Heresy is the sin of holding or proclaiming a false doctrine. In Hell, the heretics are placed in tombs that are heated red-hot in accordance with how great their heresy was.

12. Jehosaphat: The Valley of Jehosaphat was the traditionally held site of the Judgment. At the Judgment, all spirits would go to Jehosaphat and obtain their bodies.

13. Epicurus and his followers: One of Epicurus' beliefs was that there was no life after death.

25. the city: Florence.

32. Farinata: He is Manente degli Uberti, who was the leader of the Ghibellines several years before Dante's time.

47-48. had to...twice: These happened in 1248 and 1260.

52. another spirit: He is Cavalcante de' Cavalcanti.

63. Guido: Guido was Cavalcante's son, and a friend of Dante.

79-80. the Lady...fifty times: Here is a prophecy concerning Dante's exile. 'The Lady' is Proserpina, the wife of Hades; because she was identified with the moon, fifty times refers to fifty months. Within fifty months of this prophecy, Dante would be in exile.

86. Arbia: This event was the murder of many Guelfs at Montaperti.

119. Frederick II...Cardinal: Frederick II was a Holy Roman Emperor who fought with the Church for much of his rule. The Cardinal is Ottaviano degli Ubaldini, who was an ally of the Ghibellines.

Canto XI

1   Up on a high rim made of massive shattered boulders, we saw a much more terrible group of souls.

4   And because of the terrible stench that rose from the deep pit, we backed away until we found ourselves behind the cover

7   of a great tomb, which bore the inscription, "I keep Pope Anastasius, whom Phonitus persuaded from the true path."

10   "It would be best for us to wait a while before continuing, so that we might grow used to the smell and thus be able to ignore it,"

13   my master said. And I responded, "Find something for us to do, so that we do not waste precious time." And he said, "I am already thinking about it.

16   My son, past this ring of rocks are three more circles, smaller as they go down, and like the ones we have seen so far.

19   These circles hold many more damned spirits. Now, so that you may better understand when you see them, I will now explain how they are held, and why.

22   Malice is the sin that seeks to be unfair, for it is the sin meant to harm others either by violence or fraud.

This being said, because only mankind can commit the sin of   25
fraud, it is more terrible to God, and therefore those convicted of
it are lower and suffer more.

The violent are in the first circle below us, but since one can   28
use violence in three different ways, the circle is divided into
three rings.

I mean to say that the three ways are violence against God   31
himself, or to one's own self, or to one's neighbor, either to them
directly or to what is theirs, as you will now understand.

Death by violence and wounds can be done to a neighbor,   34
and also his possessions may suffer from destruction, fire, or
blackmail.

So murderers and those who harm others in malice, as well as   37
thieves and plunderers, are divided into groups in that first ring.

Also, one can do violence against himself or his own property,   40
and so those who are in the second ring repent uselessly,

for they refused the world, and gambled with their own   43
lives, and cried when they should have been happy.

Finally, one may be violent against God, if one denies him in   46
his heart, or blasphemes, and does violence against nature.

So the smallest ring holds both Sodom and Cahors and   49
everyone who speaks in strong words against God.

Now fraud, which surely goes against any good conscience,   52
is committed by a man either against a person who trusts him, or
one who does not.

Now fraud against those who do not hold you in trust is only   55
the sin of destroying the love between all men that Nature grants.
Those guilty are in the second circle below,

58 among them the hypocrites, flatterers, sorcerers and witches, falsifiers, simoniacs, thieves, barraters, pimps, and all other sorts of garbage.

61 But realize, in fraud against those trusting in you, not only is the natural love of Nature destroyed, but also love that is formed between two people that have a special trust.

64 And so it is in innermost circle of Hell, the center of the universe and of Hell, that all traitors are punished forever."

67 "Master, all your reasoning is clear to me," I said, "for it has made clear the form of this pit and those who inhabit those circles.

70 But tell me, those whom we saw, who were in that marsh, or those in the great wind, or those tormented by rain, or those that fight with their words,

73 why are they not punished here in this city if God is angry at them? And if he is not angry, then why must they be punished?"

76 And he said to me, "Why would you say such a ridiculous thing?" he said. "What other thoughts do you have?

79 Have you really forgotten how your Ethics speaks of the three sins that anger Heaven:

82 incontinence, malice, and bestiality? And also that incontinence is the sin that offends God the least?

85 So if you remember this teaching, and remember the souls in Upper Hell, who are outside this city,

88 then you will understand why they have been set apart from these, and why Heaven's punishment is least for them."

91 "O sun that clears all foggy sight, when you answer me I am as happy in knowing as I am in wondering!

But recall how you talked of usury and how it is sinful... 94
explain that to me."

"Philosophy explains, to those who understand it, time and 97
again, how Nature thrives in the way God's intellect and art
intended.

Also, if you've read Physics carefully, you will remember 100
that, not far in,

you see how man's art will mimic nature, just as a student will 103
mimic his teacher, so, in a sense, mankind's art is the grandchild
of God.

Now, from art and nature, you see, man should make his 106
living, as Genesis says.

But since usurers make their living by another path, they 109
shun Nature herself, and art, the product of Nature. He hopes to
live without them.

But come now, for we must move...now the Fishes is above 112
the horizon, and the Wain is above the Caurus.

It is a long way to where we move down the cliff." 115

CANTO XI NOTES

Still in the circle of the heretics, Dante and Virgil approach the ledge thatthey will descend; however, the stench is so foul, they are forced to retreat. They hide behind a tomb, which is holding Pope Anastasius. To make good use of their time, Virgil explains the layout of Hell: There are three more circles through which they will pass, which hold the sins of malice. The first is divided into three rings and holds the violent against others, self, and God. The next holds those who committed fraud against persons with whom they had no special relationship. The deepest part of Hell is for traitors, those who committed fraud against persons with whom they had a special relationship. Also, Dante learns why some sinners are punished outside of the city of Dis. Virgil finishes by commenting on the sin of usury.

8. Pope Anastasius...Phonitus: This phrase is obscure, and the purpose of the reference is unknown.

22. Malice: From this we learn that the sins of malice are punished in the city of Dis.

49. Sodom and Cahors: Sodom was the biblical city associated with homosexuality, and Cahors was a French city associated with usury, which will be discussed later.

79. your Ethics: Aristotle's *Nichomachean Ethics.*

82-83. incontinence, malice, and bestiality: There is some debate as to how Aristotle's divisions correspond to Hell's structure. Incontinence is generally taken to be sins punished outside of Dis (sins of excessive passion), and malice on the inside; however, bestiality could refer exclusively to violence, or otherwise to treachery (the innermost circle). Regardless, the significance of the passage is that sins of incontinence are the least offensive to God.

94. how you talked of usury: Dante is referring to Virgil mentioning Cahors. Usury is the charging of excessive interest rates on loans.

97. Philosophy: That is, Aristotle's philosophy.

112-113. Fishes...Wain...Caurus: The constellation of the Fishes (Pisces) is just rising, and the Wain (the Big Dipper) is above the Caurus (the northwest region of the sky), meaning that it is about four in the morning.

C ANTO XII

1   The place by which we meant to descend was the edge of a great cliff and was terrible in sight; the beast that lay there, too, was terrible to the eyes.

4   Like the shattered rocks that are piled on the edge of Adige on this side of Trent, because of some great earthquake or fault in the rocks,

7   so in the same way was the rock in this place shattered so that one wishing to descend could take that path.

10   This was the way to go down into the valley. There at the edge was that infamous creature of Crete,

13   who was born of a false cow; upon seeing us he started biting at himself, like one who has great fury.

16   My master said to him, "Are you so scared because you think this is the Duke of Athens, who killed you in the living world?

19   Be gone, monster…this man has not been taught by your sister how to kill you. He only comes here to see your pain."

22   And just like a bull will break free when it has received the killing stroke of a knife, and cannot move in any one direction, but thrashes about,

so I saw the Minotaur act. My ever-alert guide cried out,   25
"Quick! Run to the path, for it is easier to descend while he is so
violent!"

So we went across the shattered stones, which many times   28
shifted because they found my weight unusual.

I had a thought while descending, and he said, "You are   31
wondering about the shattered stones watched over by that
inhuman anger that I put out.

Now, the last time I descended this way, the boulders were   34
not yet shattered.

And so, if I am not mistaken, it was just shortly before the   37
entrance into Hell of that One who took out souls from Limbo

that there was a great earthquake here, so that I thought the   40
Universe had been overtaken by love

(which, some say, becomes chaos); so at that time, these   43
boulders and many others shattered.

But now look below at the boiling river of blood, in which   46
those who were violent against others stand."

O blind love and stupid rage, which make men do so many   49
foolish things in their short life, and are the cause of eternal grief!

I saw a great ditch which circled that whole place, just like   52
my guide had told me.

Between that ditch and the edge of the cliff walked many   55
centaurs with bows, just as they hunt in the living world.

Upon seeing us, they all gathered together, and arming   58
themselves, three of them came forward and stood far away.

61   One shouted, "What is it you seek by coming here? Answer from where you are or I will shoot you!"

64   My master said, "I will only talk to Chiron, and only if I may be by him; your anger has never caused you good."

67   He nudged me, saying, "This centaur is Nessus, who was killed due to Deianira and gained revenge.

70   The one in the middle looking at his own chest is the strong Chiron, who taught Achilles. The third, looking so upset, is Pholus.

73   They and thousands more ride around and shoot any soul that rises above the blood more than he is allowed."

76   By this time we were near those swift creatures. Chiron took out an arrow and used the notch to move his beard away from his mouth.

79   And when it was uncovered, he said to the other centaurs, "Have any of you noticed that he who walks behind moves whatever he touches?

82   Dead feet cannot do that." And my good guide was now close to that centaur's chest, where his human body met the body of a horse,

85   and said, "Yes, he is living, and so I must take him through this valley. It is important that he come this way…he is not here for pleasure.

88   The one that gave me this task was one who was singing 'hallelujah' in Heaven. He is not a robber, and neither am I.

91   So by the power that allows me to travel this wild path, I ask for one of your kind to travel with us

and show us where we can cross this ditch, and also carry   94
this man on his back, for he cannot fly like a spirit."

So Chiron turned to Nessus and said, "Go guide them, and   97
fight off any centaurs that block you."

With our good guide, we walked along the banks of that   100
blood-red ditch, and heard the cries of those boiling in it.

I saw many that were covered up to their foreheads, and the   103
Centaur explained, "These were kings that desired nothing but
murder and plunder.

Here they cry over their sins. Alexander and Dionysius are   106
here, who caused much grief to Sicily.

The black-haired one you see is Ezzelino, and Obizzo is the   109
blonde one; he was

killed by his son." Then I turned to the poet, and he said to   112
me, "Let him instruct you first…I will instruct you second."

Just ahead, the centaur stopped by some who were only in   115
the ditch as deep as their throats.

He pointed at a spirit that was set apart, and said, "Even in   118
God's temple this one killed the man whose heart still bleeds at
the Thames."

Then I saw some who had kept their heads above the water,   121
and some whose chests were even above. There were many there
that I recognized.

So going on, the blood was ever shallower, and we reached a   124
point where only the feet were burned. And it was in that place
that we could cross.

"You can see that on this side the river becomes shallower,"   127
the centaur said. "I will have you know

130   that on the other side it grows deeper, until it comes back around to where we saw the tyrants.

133   It is there that Justice punishes the scourge Attila, and Pyrrhus and Sextus. For all eternity it draws

136   the tears, which are caused by this boiling river, of Rinier of Corneto and Rinier Pazzo, the two that warred on the highways."

139   Then he turned, and went back to the other side.

Canto XII Notes

At the edge of the cliff, Dante and Virgil find the Minotaur. He becomes enraged, and Dante and Virgil pass by him while he is distracted. As they move down, Dante finds that the rocks are shattered; Virgil explains that they broke when Jesus entered into Hell. At the bottom of the cliff, they find a river of boiling blood, where the violent against others are found. The river is watched over by centaurs, who shoot those who try to lessen their pain. Virgil speaks with the centaur Chiron, who instructs Nessus to lead them across the river. He points out several of those punished. Finally they reach the shallowest part of the river, where they will cross, and Nessus leaves them.

2. the beast: The Minotaur, as we will find shortly.

4. shattered rocks...Adige: This refers to a landslide near Trent in northern Italy, which can be descended by foot.

11-13. creature of Crete...false cow: According to myth, the Minotaur was born after Pasiphaë, wife of King Minos, hid in a wooden cow so she could have intercourse with a bull.

16-21. Duke of Athens...your sister: Theseus was the Duke of Athens, who killed the Minotaur after receiving instructions from Ariadne, the daughter of Minos and Pasiphaë.

38. that One: Jesus, who is never mentioned by name in Hell.

41-43. love...chaos: Virgil here refers to a belief of the philosopher Empedocles that love and hate were the forces that balanced the universe. When love grew and hate diminished, the universe moved closer to the original state of chaos. Virgil attributes the earthquake to this explanation.

46. boiling river of blood: This river is Phlegethon.

46-139. THE VIOLENT AGAINST OTHERS: These are the first group of the violent, found in the eighth circle. They include those who were violent against others' bodies and possessions. Their punishment is standing in Phlegethon, a river of boiling blood. The depth at which they must stand is determined by the severity of their sin: Tyrants stand in the deepest part of the river.

67-68. Nessus...Deianira: According to tradition, Nessus tried to steal Deianira, Hercules' wife, and Hercules killed him. Before he died, Nessus told Deianira that his blood would cause Hercules to love her forever. However, when she put it on a shirt and Hercules wore it, it burned him, and he threw himself into his own funeral pyre, causing him to become a god.

88. the one: Beatrice.

106. Alexander and Dionysius: Probably Alexander the Great, and Dionysius, who ruled over Syracuse.

109-110. Ezzelino, and Obizzo: Ezzelino was a leader of the Ghibellines, and Obizzo was a violent leader of Ferrara, a city in northern Italy.

118-120. a spirit...heart still bleeds: The spirit is Guy de Montfort, who killed Henry of Cornwall in a church. The reference to his heart still bleeding probably refers to the fact that Guy de Montfort was not punished.

133-134. Attila...Pyrrhus and Sextus: This is the famous Attila the Hun. Pyrrhus is probably Pyrrhus of Epirus, and Sextus is probably Sextus Pompeius.

137-138. Rinier...Rinier...highways: The two were well-known highwaymen from Tuscany.

C ANTO XIII

1   It was even before Nessus had returned to the other side that we began to travel through a wood that had no path.

4   There were no green leaves in that forest, but only black ones. All the branches were knotted and gnarled, and they bore poisonous thorns instead of fruit.

7   Even the beasts that live between Cecina and Corneto, who much hate smooth plains, do not live in forests so thick.

10   This is where the Harpies live, those that chased out the Trojans from the Strophades by prophesying of great trouble.

13   They have great wings, and the faces and necks of humans, but they have talons on their feet and feathers on their bellies, and they cry out in the odd trees.

16   And so my kind master told me, "Before you go in farther, realize that now we are in the second ring,

19   which ends when we reach a terrible desert. So watch carefully, for you will see things that you would not believe."

22   I heard crying from all over, but I could not see who was crying, so I stopped because I did not understand.

25   I think he must have thought that I was thinking that the voices were coming from people hidden under the roots,

because he said, "If you break off a branch, that thought you have would also be broken." 28

So I put out my hand and tore off a branch from a thornbush, and it said to me, "Why are you tearing me?" 31

And I saw that the branch was bloody. And it continued, "Do you not pity me at all? 34

All of us used to be men, but now we are merely stumps. Perhaps you would have been kinder if we were only the spirits of snakes." 37

Just like wet branches hiss when they burn, with air escaping from one end, 40

so both blood and voice came from that stump, and I dropped the branch in fear. 43

My teacher said to that stump, "You tormented soul, if he would have believed what he had read in my poetry, 46

then he would not have done this thing against you. But it is the very interesting nature of your condition that forced me to tell him to do something that pains me as well. 49

But tell him who you once were, so that he can repay you by reminding living men about you." 52

So the tree said, "Your kind words compel me to answer you...please do not be offended if I take too long in explanation. 55

I am the one who was the keeper of the keys of Frederick's heart, and I was able to easily lock and unlock it, 58

so that I alone had his full trust, and I indeed was completely faithful to my position; so faithful that often I lost sleep or health over it! 61

64   But that whore, Envy, that always controls Caesar, she that is the cause of all death, and the great sin in courts,

67   she turned everyone against me. And those against me then convinced Augustus, so that all my honor became grief.

70   So that grief, in order to escape grief, caused me to act unjustly, though I was good.

73   But by my strange roots I swear to you that I never betrayed my master, who was so worthy of all honor.

76   So, if either of you ever go back to the world of the living, please bring back honor to my name, which still suffers from the attack of Envy."

79   The poet waited a while, then said to me, "Because he is silent now, take your chance to ask what you wish to know."

82   And I said, "Please ask him yourself…ask anything you think I may wish to know. I cannot, for I feel so much pity."

85   And so the poet continued, "Spirit, in order that this man may do what you request,

88   please tell us more about why you are imprisoned in these knots, and tell us if anyone can ever escape them."

91   And the trunk let out a great sigh, which became his voice: "I will answer you quickly.

94   When a spirit comes out of a man by his own hand, then Minos sends it to the seventh circle.

97   It falls here in this wood. We have no specific place, but we grow wherever Fortune has thrown us.

100   We grow like a wild plant, and the Harpies come and feed on us, causing and relieving pain at the same time.

Just like all souls here, we will one day find the flesh we left   103
on earth, but we will not wear it, for it is not right for anyone to
get back what he has thrown out.

We will drag our bodies to this wood, and they will forever   106
hang on our branches."

And we were still watching the trunk, thinking it was going   109
to continue, but at that moment we heard a loud noise,

just like a hunter is aware of beasts approaching his camp   112
when he hears the cracking of the branches that they break.

Off to the left were two scratched and naked men running so   115
quickly that they broke off all the branches they passed.

The one in front yelled, "Come quickly, Death!" The other,   118
seeing that he was falling behind, yelled to the other, "Lano, your
legs were not so fast

in the jousts at Toppo!" But, maybe because he was tired, he   121
hid behind a tree.

Just then, black dogs came rushing in as quick and ferocious   124
as greyhounds set free.

They bit him where he was resting, and taking off his limbs,   127
they dragged them away.

Then my guide took my hand and led me to the bush the   130
man had hidden behind, which was now broken and bleeding.

It said, "O, Jacopo da Santo Andrea, what was the use in using   133
me as a shield? Do you blame me for your sinful life?"

My master, standing there, said, "Who were you who say   136
your sad words through blood?"

139 And he said, "You spirits who come to watch the terrible fight that has left my branches broken,

142 please gather them together. My home was in the city of the man who made the way for John the Baptist; because of this,

145 he will always make it a sad place; and if there were not a single effigy of Mars remaining,

148 then the people there who rebuilt on the ashes left by Attila would have rebuilt in vain.

151 I made my own house the place of my hanging."

Canto XIII Notes

Dante and Virgil pass into the wood of suicides, the second ring of the seventh circle; Virgil explains that the third ring is a desert. Dante hears voices, and thinks that they are coming from spirits trapped under the trees. However, when Virgil instructs him to break off a branch, he finds that the spirits have become the trees. Dante finds Pier delle Vigne, assistant to the emperor Frederick II, who committed suicide in prison. He tells Dante that souls guilty of harm to their own body are flung into the wood and grow wherever they land; also, those spirits will not wear their body after the Judgment. Suddenly, Dante and Virgil see two men running, chased by dogs. One pauses, and is torn apart. In the process, a bush is also torn apart, and Virgil speaks with him.

1-151. THE VIOLENT AGAINST THEMSELVES: Those who committed violence against themselves are punished in the second ring of the seventh circle. There, the souls of those who committed suicide grow into trees and bushes, which are attacked by the Harpies. A second group of sinners, those who were violent against their property, are also identified; they are chased by dogs.

7-9. the beasts...so thick: This refers to Maremma, a vast swampy area in southern Tuscany.

10-12. Harpies...great trouble: In the *Aeneid,* a group of Trojans encountered Harpies (bird-like creatures with heads of women) on the Strophades, which is a group of islands. The

Harpies constantly stole or destroyed the Trojans' food, and prophesied that they would become so hungry they would eventually have to eat the plates. This prophecy drove the Trojans away.

48. my poetry: That is, because in the *Aeneid* there is an account of a bush that speaks when torn.

58-60. the keeper...Frederick's heart: This is Pier delle Vigne, who was the assistant of Emperor Frederick II. He was accused of betraying Frederick, and was imprisoned. Because of this, he killed himself.

64-69. Envy...Caesar...Augustus: Both Caesar and Augustus are titles that refer to Frederick. Pier claims it was the envy of others that caused for him to be accused and jailed.

120. Lano: This is Arcolano da Squarcia di Riccolfo Maconi, who was famous for spending his money foolishly.

133. Jacopo da Santo Andrea: According to legend, he had his house burned down when he wanted to see a fire.

142-151. my home...John...Mars...Attila: While the identity of this spirit is unknown, a few things may be determined from his account. To begin, he was from Florence, as Florence's patron had been the god Mars before converting to Christianity, when Saint Peter became the patron. He claims, though, that it was by Mars' continued worship that the rebuilding of the city after Attila the Hun destroyed it was successful. Finally, we find that, for unknown reasons, he hanged himself in his own house.

Canto XIV

1   Now love of our home city drove me to collect those scattered branches and give them back to that man, who spoke no more.

4   Going from that place, we reached the boundary between the second and third rings, and saw the terrible work Justice was doing there.

7   So that you can understand my strange words, I will explain to you that we arrived at a plain on which no green thing grows.

10   The wood we had left is like a garland enclosing that place, just in the same way that the wood was enclosed by that river. And so we walked at the edge of the boundary.

13   The ground was made of dry sand, not very much unlike the sand that Cato traveled over.

16   Everyone who has the ability to read of these things that I saw...fear the Lord's vengeance!

19   I saw an incredible number of naked spirits, crying terribly, all of whom seemed punished differently.

22   Some were lying down, some were curled into a ball and sat there, and others kept moving around.

By far, the majority of them were walking, and the smallest   25
portion were those lying down; but those lying cried more over
their punishment.

Over that desert fell flakes of fire like snow over mountains   28
when there is no wind.

Just like Alexander had his men put out flames before new   31
ones formed when fires fell on his battalion in India,

so that he ordered his men to put them out before they joined,   34

so did the flames there constantly fall, and the sand ignited   37
like tinder does when lit with flint, making the punishment even
worse.

The hands of the wretched were constantly moving, trying   40
to put out the new flames as they descended.

And I said, "Master, you who are able to conquer all things,   43
except those dumb demons that blocked our entrance here,

who is that giant, who does not care that he is being burnt by   46
the flames, and who frowns so?"

But that giant heard me talking about him, and yelled to us,   49
"I am what I was in life.

If Jove would annoy his smith by calling for many lightning   52
bolts, the smith who made the bolt that killed me,

or else annoy all other smiths in Mongibello by shouting,   55
'Help me, Vulcan!'

just like he did while at war with Phlegra, and would kill me   58
with that lightning, even then his desire for revenge would not
be satisfied."

61   And then my guide spoke stronger than I had ever heard him speak: "Capaneus, it is for your great arrogance

64   that you are punished even worse! Only your own insanity is punishment enough for your anger!"

67   But then, kindly, he turned and said to me, "He was one of seven kings that attacked Thebes; he still is quite angry

70   with God as he was in life. Now, all his sins are like jewelry on his chest.

73   Follow, but be careful not to walk on the hot sand; stay near the forest."

76   We walked in silence to a place where a small, blood-red river came out of the forest; I still shake thinking of it!

79   Just as there is a river that comes from the Bulicame, from which prostitutes drink, so this stream went across the sand.

82   The bottom and sides, as well as the boundaries, were made of stone, and so I saw that it would be our passage.

85   "Compared with all the shocking things I have shown you since we passed through that gate which ought to have been opened to us,

88   you have not seen anything as amazing as this, for this river has the power to put out all flames that fall above it."

91   This is what my guide said, and I begged him to continue, for he had given me a desire to understand.

94   "A destroyed land, Crete, is at mid-sea," he said. "Under the rule of its king, the world was once better.

97   There is a blessed mountain that has trees and good water; it is called Ida. But now it dies like one does from age.

At one time, Rhea chose it as the cradle for her son, to hide   100
him; when he cried, she had her servants run to him.

In that place there is an Old Man, who has his back turned   103
to Damietta and looks towards Rome as though it were a mirror.

The Man's head is made of gold, his arms and chest are silver,   106
and the rest of his torso is brass.

His legs are iron, except for his right foot, which is made of   109
clay; that foot holds more of his weight than the left.

Every part of his body, except the head of gold, is cracked.   112
From that crack, tears fall down and drip through the cavern
floor,

and, running into this place, join to form the Acheron, and   115
the Styx, and the Phlegethon, and eventually to this small river.

They end where Hell ends, Cocytus. But because you will see   118
this, I will not tell you about it now."

And I asked, "But if this is true, why is it that we have only   121
seen this river now?"

He replied, "Now remember that Hell is round, and that it is   124
very deep and large. Recall how in descending we have always
travelled to the left.

We have not yet gone all the way around the circle, so it   127
should not surprise you when you see something new."

And I spoke again, "Master, where is Phlegethon, and where   130
is Lethe? You have not even spoken of the second, but you said
that the tears form the first."

"I am very happy," he said, "that you ask all these questions;   133
yet, you already knew the answer to one when you saw this
boiling river, for that is Phlegethon.

136   And you will see Lethe, but not in Hell. Rather, you will see it in the place where repentance washes away the guilt of sinners."

139   Then he said, "Now it is time for us to leave this wood. Be careful to walk close to me, and stay on the stone boundary of this river, where the sand does not burn

142   and the flames that fall are put out."

Canto XIV Notes

Dante collects the broken branches of the unknown man, and then continues on. He and Virgil arrive at a vast desert, where the violent against God are punished. There is a constant downpour of fire, which burns the sinners and the sand. There they see the giant Capaneus. They travel along the edge of the wood and find a red river that flows from it, which has a stone border. Virgil explains that the river, as well as all the others in Hell, originate from the tears of the Old Man of Crete. Virgil shows that the walls on the border of the red river are safe from the fire, and will be used as a path.

4-142. THE VIOLENT AGAINST GOD: The violent against God are punished in this third ring of the seventh circle. The ring is a large desert upon which flames fall constantly. The degree to which spirits may move about to avoid the flames depends on their sin; those moving about are the homosexuals, those curled up are the usurers, those forced to lie down are the blasphemers.

13-14. dry sand...Cato: Cato led his army through the Sahara desert during the war between Pompey and Julius Caesar.

31-36. Just like Alexander...put them out: This refers to a letter that was believed to be written by Alexander, in which he stated that in India flames fell from the sky, and he had his men put them out.

52-60. Jove...Phlegra: Capaneus (who is the giant) claims that even if Jove (that is, Jupiter) ordered for many lightning bolts to be made, as he did at the battle at Phlegra, then Zeus still would be unable to get revenge against Capaneus. Of course, as Capaneus is now damned to Hell, this is all nonsense.

79. Bulicame: The Bulicame is a spring that is colored red because it contains sulfur.

100. Rhea...her son: It was said that Rhea hid her son, Jupiter, on Ida because her husband, Saturn, ate his children to ensure that none of them would take his place.

103-105. Old Man...Damietta...Rome: To begin, it must be understood that the Old Man is basically an invention of Dante. It resembles the statue about which Nebuchadnezzar dreamed (recorded in the book of Daniel). The statue has its back facing Damietta, a city in Egypt, and its front faces faces Rome. Interpretations of the symbolisms of the Old Man are too varied and disagreed upon to be mentioned here. However, it is stated that the tears that flow from the Man's eyes form the rivers of Hell.

136. Lethe...repentance washes away: The place is Purgatory.

Canto XV

1   Now we walked forward on one of the stone sides of the river, the mist of it shielding the water and shore from fire.

4   Just as the Flemings have built walls to hold in the sea between Wissant and Bruges for fear of flooding,

7   and the Paduans built walls along Brenta to protect their towns from the great spring floods from Carentana,

10   so were these walls, though they were not very high or wide.

13   By this time we were so far from the wood that I would not have been able to see it even if I had looked for it.

16   We found a group of spirits around that bank, and stared at us as men do

19   beneath the dark of a new moon. They squinted their eyes as a tailor does to see the eye of his needle.

22   And when they looked harder, one of them recognized me, and grabbing my cloak yelled, "How wonderful!"

25   When that spirit grabbed me I looked hard at his burned body so that even his destroyed face could not hide

28   his identity from me. Lowering my face to see his, I said, "Are you here, Ser Brunetto?"

And he said, "My son, please do not mind if Brunetto Latini 31
stays with you awhile and allows his group to move on."

I said, "I pray that you would with all my being! I will stay 34
with you awhile, if my guide so allows me."

And he replied, "Son, if anyone in this group stops walking 37
for even a moment, then he is cursed to lie down for a hundred
years, unable to shield himself from the fires.

So keep walking…I will follow you down here for awhile, 40
but then I must return to my group as we go crying over our
eternal suffering."

I did not dare to go down to his level, but I did walk with my 43
head bent like one in honor.

And he said, "What destiny or turn of chance brings you 46
here before your last day, and who is this man who guides you?"

"In the sunlit life above," I started, "before my life was over I 49
went astray in a valley.

It was only yesterday that I turned from it, but being lost 52
nonetheless, this guide appeared to me, to take me home by this
route."

And he said, "If you follow your star, you will certainly reach 55
the good place, if I have judged you correctly in life.

And seeing that the heavens favored you, I would have 58
helped you in your work, if I had not died so soon.

But that terrible, hateful people that in ancient times came 61
from Fiesole, and still act like mountain people,

will be your enemy because of what you do. But that is 64
proper, for figs do not bear their good fruit with bitter apples.

67 For a long time the world has called them blind; they are envious, proud, and greedy.

70 Make sure that you do not follow their ways. Fortune will honor you greatly; both sides will surely desire to kill you, but be sure to keep grass far away from the goat.

73 Let the beasts of Fiesole consume themselves, and leave the plant be so that it may grow from their atrociousness

76 in that place where the children of those Romans who remained good when the place became corrupt may live again."

79 "If my desire was done," I said to Ser Brunetto, "then you would be among the living and not the dead.

82 I still remember your kind, paternal role, when, in the world above, you often

85 taught me how man becomes eternal; so, while I am still living, I hope you can always hear gratitude in my words.

88 I will write down what you have told me of my life, and will keep it with other text, so that one Lady can interpret, if I reach her.

91 But I hope that you can see one thing as obvious: As long as I do nothing against my conscience, I am prepared for anything Fortune does to me.

94 Already I have heard the prophecy you have given me, so let Fortune do her job just as peasants do theirs."

97 My master turned his head to the right and said to me, "You have done well in considering what you have heard."

100 But regardless of this, I continued to talk to Ser Brunetto, and I asked him who of his group are famous and good.

And he told me, "It is good for me to mention some, but it is   103
better to leave some unmentioned. We do not have much time
to talk.

To be brief, know that my group includes many clerics and   106
famous, intelligent men, who all are guilty of the same sin.

That sad group includes Priscian and Francesco d'Accorso.   109
You can also see, if you have any desire to see such a wretched
man,

the Servant of Servants who came from the Arno back to the   112
banks of the Bacchiglione, and was stained by sin there.

I would continue, but I cannot, for beyond I see a new smoke   115
coming up from the sand,

where there is a group with which I do not belong. Let my   118
Tesoro, in which I am still alive, be useful for you; that is all I
request."

Then he turned and seemed like one of those who run across   121
fields to win Verona's green cloth; and indeed,

I thought he would win, and not lose.   124

CANTO XV NOTES

Dante and Virgil continue onward by walking on top of one of the stone sides of the river, Phlegethon; the steam rising from it protects them from the falling flames. As they walk, they see a group of sinners walking around near them, and one of them recognizes Dante. It is Brunetto Latini, who was a sort of father figure to Dante. They go on talking for awhile, and Latini also prophesies concerning Dante's coming exile. Latini mentions some of the others in his group (who are the homosexuals), and then races off.

4-9. Flemings, etc.: Dante compares the river's walls to the walls built by the Flemings and Paduans to prevent flooding.

29. Ser Brunetto: This is Brunetto Latini, an important political figure in Florence. He is here identified as a homosexual, though there is no historical evidence that this is the case.

55. your star: Possibly referring to Gemini, the constellation under which Dante was born, though it could refer to Dante's talent.

61-63. terrible, hateful people: It was a legend at the time that when Florence was built, Fiesolians also settled there and mixed with the Romans. Florentines of the time regarded the Fiesolians as uncivilized, hence the 'mountain' reference.

65-66. figs...bitter apples: That is to say, good people perform good works, and evil people perform evil works, so the two cannot coexist.

73-78. the plant...Romans: Latini here essentially attributes all of the strife of Florence to the presence of the descendants of the Fiesolians.

109. Priscian and Francesco d'Accorso: Priscian was a Latin grammarian, and d'Accorso was a jurist just before Dante's times.

112. Servant of Servants: This is Andrea de' Mozzi, called 'servant of servants' ironically, because 'servant of the servants of God' is used to refer to the pope, and de' Mozzi was transferred by Boniface VIII to be bishop in Vicenza, near Bacchiglione, on account of his various crimes.

119. Tesoro: This is Latini's famous poem, translated as 'Treasure.'

121-122. Verona's green cloth: There was a tradition in Verona where young men would race in a field; the winner would be awarded green cloth, and the loser would have to carry back a rooster.

CANTO XVI

1   When I reached the place where one can hear the murmur of water as it falls to the next circle, sounding like a beehive,

4   I saw three spirits running, leaving their group under the rain of punishment.

7   They were coming toward us, each of them yelling, "Stop! We can tell from your clothes that you are from our bad country!"

10   What terrible scars I saw on their bodies, both new and old, caused by the fire! I still hurt to recall it.

13   My master heard their call and said to me, "Wait. We must honor these ones.

16   In fact, if this were not the place where fire falls, I would say that it would be more proper for you to run to them."

19   As soon as we stopped, they started calling out again. When they reached us, they began walking around in a circle.

22   Just like champions, naked and anointed, will always study their weapon and grip before they begin fighting,

25   so each of them made sure that his face was always toward me by turning his head the direction opposite the path of his feet as he walked.

"If the desolation of this sandy place and our disgusting   28
appearance make us unbearable,

then at least let our earthly fame compel you to tell us who   31
you are, you whose living feet walk through Hell so confidently.

The man that walks before me in this circle, who is naked   34
with peeling skin, was much greater than you think:

He was called Guido Guerra, the grandson of Gualdrada; in   37
life he was famous for both his politics and his war.

The one behind me is Tegghiaio Aldobrandi, a man whose   40
words other men should have listened to.

I, who have the same punishment, am Jacopo Rusticucci.   43
Surely, it was my savage wife that was most responsible for my
death."

If I would have had a way to protect myself from the fire, I   46
would have gone down to them...and I think my master would
have allowed it.

However, since I would have been burned, my fear overcame   49
my good intentions that made me desire to embrace them.

Then I said, "Your punishment has not created disgust in me,   52
but rather great sadness,

as soon as my master told me what kind of men you were,   55
you men of great worth.

For I am from the same city as you; indeed, I have always   58
been glad to tell others about you and your works, and also to
hear others tell of them.

I must leave this terrible place and go to the sweet apples   61
that my guide has promised me; but first, I must go to the center
of Hell."

64   "Let your soul be with your body for a long time, and may you see great fame," he then answered,

67   "but tell us, is our city still filled with kindness and honor as it was while we lived? Or are they gone?

70   Guglielmo Borsiere, who just recently has come to be punished with us, and walks with our group, has greatly saddened us with the reports he brings."

73   "What can I say of Florence! Already, newcomers and scams have brought gluttony and arrogance, and Florence weeps for it!"

76   So I turned up my head and cried. The three men stared at each other as men do when they hear a terrible truth.

79   "If you can always answer so quickly," all three said, "then bless you who can speak so clearly at will.

82   If you are able to leave this dark land, and see the good stars when you return, when you are finally able to recall this experience and say, 'I was,'

85   please remember us." This said, they broke their circle, and ran with legs that were like wings.

88   They disappeared faster than a man can say, "Amen." My master thought it was time to leave,

91   and so I followed. It was not before long that the waters grew so loud that we could not have been able to hear each other speak.

94   Even as that river which first takes an eastern course from Mount Viso along the left side of the Apennines

97   (which, at the top, they call Acquacheta before it falls into its valley, and which is called by a different name beyond Forli),

sounds so loud above San Benedetto dell'Alpe as it falls as   100
though it were a thousand rivers,

    so we heard that black water roar as it fell down a steep slope;   103
indeed, it was loud enough to cause pain.

    Around my waist I had a cord to hold my cloak in place.   106
(I had thought earlier that I might have been able to catch that
leopard in the wood with it.)

    After I had taken it off, as my guide had told me to do, I gave   109
it to him all coiled up.

    He turned to his right and threw it down into the pit some   112
distance from the edge.

    "Surely some unusual thing must answer," I thought to   115
myself, "to this odd sign that my master watches so closely."

    How much care a man must take when he stands beside one   118
who can read his thoughts and not just his actions!

    He said, "Soon will arise what I am waiting for and what you   121
have thought about. Soon you will see it."

    Now when a man is told a truth that he is sure is a lie, it is   124
better for him to be quiet as long as he can and indicate that he is
embarrassed to think such a thing, even though he has no fault.

    But I cannot be quiet at this point; reader, I swear by the   127
words of this Comedy, and may my words be read for many years,

    that up through the dark air I saw a figure, enough to shock   130
even the bravest man,

    like one rising up from the water where he went to loose an   133
anchor stuck on a reef, or something else in the sea,

    who then comes back up on his feet.   136

CANTO XVI NOTES

Moving onward, Dante find three men from Florence, Guido Guerra, Tegghiaio Aldobrandi, and Jacopo Rusticucci, all punished in Hell for homosexuality. They walk in a circle as they converse with Dante; he tells them that he must continue to the center of Hell, and also of the declining condition of Florence. The three depart, and Dante and Virgil continue to the end of the river, where they find a large pit. Virgil tosses the rope from Dante's cloak over the edge, and a terrifying beast arises from the darkness.

9. our bad country: That is, Florence.

20-21. they began...circle: Recall that any sinner who stops moving here is punished by lying down for one hundred years.

37-39. Guido Guerra: Guido was a prominent leader of the Guelfs, who was a member of the party after their exile and through their regaining power in Florence a few decades before the events of the *Inferno*.

40-42. Tegghiaio Aldobrandi...words: Tegghiaio was also a Guelf; he had advised against the expedition that brought about a terrible defeat at Montaperti.

43-45. Jacopo Rusticucci...my savage wife: Another Guelf. It would seem that he blames his wife for his becoming a homosexual.

70. Guglielmo Borsiere: Little is known about him, other than he was a member of the court, was a peacemaker, and arranged marriages.

73. newcomers and scams: Evidently, Dante is referring to rich emigrants to Florence, who brought their evil ways with them.

84. 'I was': That is, after Dante's travel is over and when he is recording his experiences.

94-99. that river: Dante is here comparing the sound of the waterfall he is approaching to the sound of the Acquacheta, which was called the Montone after it had passed Forli.

100-102. thousand rivers: That is, the noise heard at the end of Phlegethon is similar to the noise of the Acquacheta above San Benedetto dell'Alpe, which was a monastery.

Canto XVII

1   "See, the beast with a pointed tail, who flies over mountains and destroys weapons and walls. See the beast with a stench that fills all the world!"

4   So my guide started, and then motioned for the beast to come onto land, closer to the end of the path we were walking.

7   And it rested, that symbol of fraud, with its head and chest on the wall, but did not set down its tail.

10   It had a face just like a man's, truly, that part of its appearance was beautiful; yet all the rest of its body was like a snake's;

13   it had two paws, and hair on its arms up to its armpits; its back and chest and its legs all had thick knots and curls of hair.

16   Indeed, no Turks or Tartars ever created fabrics that were more colorful, nor had Arachne ever made a more colorful web.

19   Just as a boat will sometimes sit partially on land and partially in water, and just as in the land of the guzzling Germans

22   the beaver will stand in that way when preparing to fight, so that beast lay on the stone.

25   Its tail was shaking in the abyss, and it kept putting up the fork of its tail, which carries poison like a scorpion.

My guide said, "Now we must go slightly out of our way,   28
until we reach the place where the beast crouches.

And so we went down on the right side and walked ten paces   31
along that wall in order to protect ourselves from the sand and
fire.

When we reached the beast, I saw just a bit off, some sinners   34
sitting in the sand.

And my master said to me, "So that you many have a complete   37
understanding of this ring, go and see what they are doing.

But do not talk with them long; while you are gone, I will   40
talk with this beast, and see if it will allow us to ride its back.

So I went on, alone, closer to the edge of the seventh circle,   43
where these depressed people sat.

Their eyes were filled with great depression; their hands   46
protected their one side, then the other, sometimes from the fire
and sometimes from the sand,

just as dogs do in summer if they are muzzled, and they are   49
bit by fleas or gnats.

When I looked at all the ones burned by the flames, I   52
recognized none of them, but I noticed

that each had a money bag hanging from his neck, each a   55
special color and bearing a special emblem, and their eyes seemed
constantly drawn to these pouches.

Looking around, I saw a yellow purse with azure that bore   58
the face of a lion.

Then, looking farther, I saw one that was blood-red, with a   61
butter-white goose.

64   And one man, who had a white pouch with a pregnant blue cow on it, said, "Why are you here?

67   Go away…since you still live, do not forget that my neighbor, Vitaliano, will sit here on my left.

70   All these men are Florentines, but I am a Paduan; I hear them shouting in my ear, 'Let the cavalier, the one with the pouch

73   bearing three goats, come!'" Then he stopped, and stuck out his tongue, like an ox licking his nose.

76   Afraid that staying any longer would only anger my master, who told me to be brief, I went away from those tired souls.

79   I found my guide, who already was sitting on the back of that beast. He said, "Be strong and courageous now,

82   for this is the way we must go down. You will sit in front; I will sit between you and the tail, so that it cannot hit you.

85   Just as one who feels like malaria is near, and shivers, already his nails blue, the darkness enough to frighten him,

88   so I was when I heard him speak. But then, I feared shame; indeed, this is what makes a servant brave before his kind master.

91   I sat down on those enormous shoulders, and I tried to say (but my voice did not come out as I thought), "Please hold me tight!"

94   But he, who many times before had helped me in dangers, grabbed on to me as soon as I climbed on. He said,

97   "Now, Geryon, move; be sure to make your circles wide and your landing slow; remember the weight you now carry."

100   Just like a boat that sets off first backs up, so that beast did, and he flew into the air. And when he had left the cliff,

he turned in a circle and, extending his tail, curled it like an 103
eel, and gathered the air with his wings.

I do not even think Phaethon was more afraid when he let 106
his reigns free, scorching the sky,

nor Icarus when he could feel his wings coming off from the 109
melting wax, and his father shouting, "That is the wrong way!"

than I when I saw nothing around me except air and the 112
beast.

Very slowly he descended in a spiral, but I could only feel 115
the wind.

Even then I could hear the river to my right below us, so I 118
looked down.

But then I grew even more afraid of falling, for I saw fire and 121
heard crying, so I trembled and held tighter.

And now I saw what before I had missed: that our path was 124
bringing us closer to torment on every side.

Just as a falcon, having flown for many hours straight and 127
finding no prey or other bird,

will descend in a hundred circles rather than all at once, and 130
will in anger sit far from his master, so that he says, "Ah, he gives
up already!"

so Geryon did once he had finally let us off at the bottom of 133
the cliff. And once we left his back,

he shot back up like an arrow from a bow. 136

CANTO XVII NOTES

As Dante and Virgil wait at the edge of the cliff, Geryon, a horrific beast, arises from the depths. As Virgil speaks with Geryon, Dante goes to speak with a group of sinners sitting in the sand nearby. They are the usurers, the final group of the violent against God, money lenders that charged excessive interest rates. Dante sees they all have moneybags around their necks. One speaks to him briefly, telling Dante to leave, and then sticks out his tongue. Dante returns to find Virgil sitting on Geryon's back; he also climbs on, and Geryon begins his descent in wide circles.

1. the beast: It is Geryon, a monster from mythology, who was killed by Hercules. There are many differing descriptions of its appearance in classical literature, and Dante's description is unique.

16-18. Turks....Tartars...Arachne: The Turks and Tartars were the best weavers of Dante's time. Arachne was a weaver who was turned into a spider by the goddess Minerva after she lost to Arachne in a weaving contest. Geryon's hair is extremely colorful.

58-60. yellow...azure...lion: The emblem of the Gianfigliazzi family, members of the Black Guelfs.

61-63. blood-red...butter-white goose: The emblem of the Obriachi family, members of the Ghibellines.

64-69. one man...Vitaliano: Probably Reginaldo degli

Scrovegni. He is waiting for another usurer, likely Vitaliano del Dente, to join him in Hell.

70-73. the cavalier...three goats: Just as he is awaiting the arrival of Vitaliano, the Florentine usurers are waiting for another Florentine, Giovanni Buiamonte, a member of the Ghibellines.

106-108. Phaethon...the sky: Phaethon was the son of Helios, the sun god, who drove the chariot of the sun over the earth every day. When Phaethon drove the chariot one day, he lost control and scorched the earth and sky. He was eventually struck down by Zeus.

109-111. Icarus: Icarus' father, Daedalus, had crafted wings from feathers and wax, which allowed him to fly. Despite his father's warnings, Icarus flew too close to the sun, causing the wax to melt; he fell into the sea and drowned.

Canto XVIII

1   In Hell, there is a circle called Malebolge, made of stone the color of iron, just like the wall that surrounds it.

4   In the center of that evil place is an abyss, a massive pit; I will tell you of its form in due time.

7   So this circle, between that pit and the wall, is divided into ten valleys.

10   Just like how many moats surround a castle to protect it, and so give the appearance of a set of circles,

13   so were the valleys in that place; and just as castles have many bridges across the moats,

16   so did the bridges here go across the ditches from the large cliff to the central pit, which cuts them off.

19   This was the place where we found ourselves when Geryon had left us; the poet moved to the left, and I walked behind him.

22   To my right I saw new miseries, new tortures and new torturers, in the first ditch of Malebolge.

25   In the bottom, naked sinners were moving, those on our side of the middle were facing us; those on the other side were moving the same way we were, but much faster,

just as how the Romans, in the year of Jubilee, made a plan to   28
have the great crowds move across the bridge,

those traveling to St. Peter's on one side, those heading   31
towards the Mount on the other.

On both sides of the ditch I saw horned demons with massive   34
whips, who lashed the spirits' backs.

Indeed, just one stroke made the sinners keep moving ahead!   37
No sinner dared wait for a second or third.

And as I progressed, my eyes met those of another, and I   40
exclaimed, "I have seen this sinner before!"

And so I stopped to study his face, and my guide stopped too,   43
and allowed me to take a few steps back.

That abused soul thought he could hide himself by lowering   46
his face, but it did no good. I said, "You with your head

bent low! If I correctly see you, you are Venedico   49
Caccianemico; how did you come to deserve this punishment?"

And he replied, "I do not wish to speak; it is your plain words,   52
which remind of the old world, that compel me to speak.

I was the one who led Ghisolabella to do the Marquis' will,   55
however they retell that disgusting story.

Indeed, I am not the only Bolognese weeping here. Truly,   58
this place is so full of us that we are more numerous than those
that say 'Sipa!'

between the Savena and Reno. If you doubt this, just   61
remember our greedy hearts."

As he spoke, a demon whipped him and cried out, "Keep   64
moving, you pimp! There are no women here for you to sell!"

67   Again I joined my guide; only a few steps ahead we came to a place where a bridge went out.

70   We easily climbed up, and turning to the right we left those spirits to their never-ending circling.

73   And when we reached the part of that bridge which was cut out for the lashed to circle underneath, my guide said, "Stop, and look at the rest of the spirits,

76   for you haven't seen their faces yet, because they had been moving the same direction as us."

79   Out from that old bridge we looked at those approaching us on the other side; they too were being whipped.

82   And my good master, though I had not spoken aloud, said, "Look at that one who does not cry a single tear;

85   how he still tries to look like a king! He is Jason, who with great cunning and courage stole the golden ram from the men of Colchis.

88   He travelled later to the island of Lemnos after its women, strong and unforgiving, killed all the men.

91   With loving words and looks, he seduced Hypsipyle, that girl who before had deceived all the other women.

94   But then he abandoned her, pregnant; it is this guilt that punishes him, and he is punished as revenge for Medea, too.

97   Along with him all seducers go: This is all you need know of this valley and those in it."

100   We were already in the place where the bridge ended onto the second wall, on which the next bridge starts.

Now we heard the whining of the people in the second ditch, and heard them snorting and beating themselves.

And a disgusting steam of stench rose from below and stuck to the walls, encrusting them with mold, and it was like a war on eyes and noses.

But the bottom was so deep that we could not see into it except from the bridge's highest point.

So that is where we went, and we saw in the ditch people plunged in human excrement; indeed, it seemed like it were poured there from all the world's toilets.

And as I looked around in that disgusting place, I saw a man whose face was so covered with shit that one could not tell if he were a priest or a layman.

He howled up, "Why do you stare more at me than the others here, who are just as filthy?" And I said, "Because, if I remember correctly,

I have seen you before with dry hair. And so I watch you more than the others, Alessio Interminei of Lucca!"

Then he beat his forehead and continued, "I am here because of flatteries that overflowed from my mouth."

And my guide said, "Lean out a little more, so that you can see the face

of that repulsive and disgusting tramp scratching herself with shitty nails, constantly crouching and standing.

She is Thais, the whore who answered her lover's question, 'Are you very grateful?' with 'Very? No; incredibly!'

But now we have seen more than enough of this place."

103

106

109

112

115

118

121

124

127

130

133

136

Canto XVIII Notes

Dante and Virgil now find themselves in Malebolge, a circle that slopes downward toward a central pit. There are ten deep ditches (called bolgia) which circle around the pit, with several bridges that connect the walls that surround the ditches. This is the place where simple fraud is punished. In the first ditch, Dante finds pimps and seducers whipped by demons; the pimps are walking counterclockwise, and the seducers are walking clockwise. Dante briefly speaks with a sinner there before moving onto the bridge; from there, he and Virgil are able to see the seducers: Dante recognizes one, and Virgil points out another.

22-99. THE PIMPS AND SEDUCERS: In the first bolgia, or ditch, of Malebolge, pimps and seducers are punished. They are forced to walk around the circle of the ditch as they are whipped by demons.

28-33. year of Jubilee: In 1300, Pope Boniface VIII declared special forgiveness of sins to those who visited certain sites in Rome for several days. This caused a massive influx of people having to cross over the Tiber River. They would pass over to travel to St. Peter's Basilica, and could cross back over again to the Mount on the other side, Monte Giordano. In order to control traffic, the now-common practice of 'walking on the right' was instituted. In this first ditch in Malebolge, the same rule applies: The pimps, who are walking counterclockwise, travel on the side farther from the center of Hell, and the seducers, who are walking clockwise, travel on the side closer to the center of Hell.

49. Venedico Caccianemico: He sold his sister to Obizzo d'Este (who was mentioned as being punished for violence in Canto 12).

55-57. I...led Ghisolabella: Ghiso was the name of Venedico's sister (Ghiso la bella would mean 'Ghiso the beautiful').

60-61. 'Sipa!': Prostitution and seduction were so common in Bologna that Venedico claim that there are more Bolognese in Hell than on earth: 'Sipa' is Bolognese for 'yes,' and the city is situated between the Savena and Reno rivers.

85-87. Jason...golden ram: In the famous story, Jason and the Argonauts sought out the golden fleece (golden ram).

88-93. Lemnos...Hypsipyle...deceived all the other women: The women of Lemnos, an island near modern-day Turkey, failed to worship Aphrodite, so she made them all smell so awful their husbands slept with women from the mainland. In anger, they killed all the men in their sleep, and made Hypsipyle, the daughter of the king, Thoas, their queen. However, Hypsipyle had secretly saved her father by hiding him in a chest and sending it out to sea. When Jason and the Argonauts arrived, they slept with the women of the island, and Jason fathered twins with Hypsipyle. While still pregnant, he and the Argonauts left the island.

95-96. revenge for Medea: Medea was the daughter of the king of Colchis, where the golden fleece was located. Jason seduced Medea, and she aided him greatly in acquiring the fleece. Eventually, they fled the island together, married, and had two children; however, Jason abandoned her, causing her to kill his new wife as well as her own children.

103-139: THE FLATTERERS: The second ditch of Malebolge is reserved for flatterers, and is filled with human excrement.

123. Alessio Interminei: Nothing is known about him other than that his family was allied with the White Guelfs.

133-135. Thais...'Very? No; incredibly!': Thais was a character in the play 'Eunuchus' by Terence. Thais' lover sent her a slave as a gift, and then another servant to ask if she was grateful for the gift. For a very long time she was well-known as an example of a flatterer.

Canto XIX

1   O Simon Magus, O followers, you who foul the things of God, which ought to be good,

4   and ruin them for money, now the trumpet of Judgment has sounded for you: You are kept in the third ditch!

7   We had already reached the part of the bridge that was directly above the middle of the next tomb.

10   O Greatest Wisdom, how amazing is the art of the earth and heavens, and the evil world; how fairly your power delivers Justice!

13   I saw along the sides of that pit and in the bottom, holes in the rock, all the same size, and round.

16   And indeed, they appeared no larger or smaller than those holes in lovely San Giovanni, which are made for baptizers;

19   not long ago, I broke one open to save a man drowning; let all men read this so they understand.

22   From each hole rose up the legs of a sinner, down to their thighs; the rest of their bodies were in the holes.

25   All of them had the soles of their feet on fire; they struggled so greatly that they would have broken strongly-braided ropes.

Just as things covered in oil burn only on the outside, so they   28
burned from their heels to their toes.

"Master, who is that one that shows punishment by struggling   31
more than his friends," I said, "and is burned with a redder flame?"

And he said to me, "If you would wish me to carry you down   34
the less steep bank, you can learn from him his name and sins."

I responded, "All that would please you pleases me; you are   37
my master; you know that I do your will, and you know even
what I do not say."

So we came to the fourth bank; we went to the left and   40
descended into the narrow, pocketed ditch.

My good master did not let me down until we reached the   43
place where that sinner was crying out with his legs.

"Whatever you are, upside down, sad soul, planted in the   46
ground," I began, "speak to us if you are able."

I was like a friar hearing the confession of an assassin, who,   49
once he knows he is doomed, calls back the friar to put off his
death a little longer.

He cried out, "Are you already here, are you already here,   52
Boniface? The prophesies were off by several years.

Are you already satisfied with the money you acquired by   55
falsely marrying the lovely lady and then destroying her?"

And I became like one who stands confused, as if mocked,   58
and at a loss for words.

Virgil said, "Say quickly, 'I am not Boniface, I am not the   61
man you think I am,'" and I replied as he instructed.

64   So that spirit twisted; sighing with a voice full of tears he said to me, "What do you want?

67   If you really want to know who I am, and you came into this ditch just to find out, then know that I bore the great mantle;

70   but truly I was a son to the she-bear, so greedy to make her cubs wealthy that I pocketed money on earth; now I pocket myself here.

73   Beneath my head are all the others that were simonists before I, pressed farther into the holes of the rock.

76   I will also be pushed down when the man I thought you were comes here, when I accused you in haste.

79   But I have been upside down with my feet burning for a longer time than he will be:

82   After him will come another man, a horrid shepherd of terrible deeds, from the west; he will cover both of us.

85   He will be another Jason (the one we read about in Maccabees). As his king was too indulgent to him, so the king of France will be to this new man."

88   I do not know if now I became too harsh, for I responded with these words: "Now tell me, how much money did

91   our Lord demand from Saint Peter before giving him the keys to heaven? Surely, all he asked was, 'Follow me.'

94   Peter and the others took no money from Matthias when he took the place of the evil soul.

97   So stay right where you are, for you deserve your punishment; keep your money, which made you bold against Charles.

And were I not so restricted by my highest respect for the   100
keys, which you were happy to hold,

I would use stronger words, for your crimes hurt the entire   103
world, destroying the good and aiding the evil.

The Evangelist spoke of shepherds like you when he saw the   106
one who sits on the water whoring with kings;

who has seven heads, and took strength from her ten horns   109
while virtue was pleasing to her husband.

You have made money your god, so what is the difference   112
between you and an idolater, except that he worships one god,
and you a hundred?

Constantine, it was not your conversion, but that money that   115
the first rich father took from you, that has been the root of so
much evil!"

So while I was singing this to him, he was kicking violently,   118
though I am not sure whether it was anger or his conscience.

I truly believe this pleased my leader, for he stood with a   121
very contented smile while I spoke these true words.

So he seized me with both arms, and lifted me up, and carried   124
me back the way we had come.

He did not tire of holding me, but carried me all the way to   127
the top of the bridge between the fourth and fifth ridges.

There he put me down gently on the rough and steep ridge,   130
which even goats would have trouble crossing.

From there I could see another ditch.   133

CANTO XIX NOTES

Dante and Virgil are now at the top of the bridge over the third ditch, where simonists (also called simoniacs) are held. The walls and bottom of the ditch are filled with pits in which the sinners are held upside down. Dante notices one sinner struggling more than others, and he descends with Virgil. The sinner is Pope Nicholas III, who thinks Dante is Pope Boniface VIII. Nicholas predicts the imminent death of Boniface, and the death of Pope Clement V soon after. Dante begins a strong verbal attack against the sin of simony, and they depart after.

1-123. THE SIMONISTS: Simony is the use of church artifacts, offices, and other sacred things for earthly gain. Simonists are punished in the third ditch of Malebolge in a clever irony: They are stuck upside-down in pits, which are described by Dante as resembling a type of baptismal font, which is an inversion of the method of baptism; in addition, their feet are on fire, mimicking the anointing of the disciples at Pentecost, when the Holy Spirit appeared as tongues of fire above their heads.

1. Simon Magus: Acts 8 records the story of Simon Magus, a sorcerer who was converted to Christianity. Seeing that the apostles were able to perform great miracles, he asks how much he must pay to receive the power of the Holy Spirit. Peter rebukes him, saying that it is a gift of God, and cannot be bought. Fittingly, simony is named after him.

16-21. San Giovanni: To begin, Dante is comparing the appearance of the holes to the appearance of a type of baptismal font he had seen at San Giovanni, a church. The details of him having destroyed one is much debated. However, the simplest explanation is that a child became lodged in one of the fonts and was drowning, and Dante broke open the wooden cover to save the child. Regardless, it would appear that some event did occur, and that Dante is explaining the cause of his actions.

52-57. Boniface...lovely lady: This sinner believes that Dante is Pope Boniface VIII, who is expected to arrive in Hell in the next few years. The 'lovely lady' is the church: Boniface, as with all others who are punished and will be punished here, used the church for personal profit.

69. great mantle: The mantle of the papacy, which indicates the sinner was pope. The next few lines reveal his identity.

70-71. she-bear...my cubs: 'She-bear' in Italian is 'orsa,' indicating that this is Pope Nicholas III, who had the family name of 'Orsini.' His cubs are his offspring and family, whom he tried to make wealthy through his simony.

73-78. all the others...the man I thought you were: All previous popes guilty of simony are, in fact, deeper down in the same hole. Whenever another is sent into Hell, he is plunged into the hole and pushes the others farther down. Nicholas is waiting for Boniface to be the next.

82-84. another: Pope Clement V.

85-87: another Jason...king of France: In apocryphal texts, Jason was a Jew who bribed his king, thus obtaining the high priesthood. In the same way, Clement acquired his office through simony with Philip, the king of France.

94-96: Matthias...evil soul: Matthias replaced Judas Iscariot following his death.

98-99. bold against Charles: After Nicholas' plan to have his niece marry king Charles I of Sicily failed, he supported a conspiracy against Charles, which eventually led to a successful rebellion in Sicily.

106. The Evangelist: The Apostle John.

107-111. that one...seven heads...ten horns: This is a reference to part of the vision of Revelation of a woman sitting on a beast with seven heads and ten horns (Dante was incorrect in stating it was the woman with the heads and horns). The woman is a symbol of corruption in the church. Dante now states that popes guilty of simony are fulfillments of the vision.

115-117. Constantine...first rich father: This strange statement refers to what was known as the 'Donation of Constantine,' which purportedly occurred in the early 300s. It was believed that Constantine, after adopting Christianity as the official religion of the Roman Empire, granted his God-given authority over Italy to Pope Sylvester, 'the first rich father,' and to all popes to follow him. With this power and wealth, simony and other evils could be easily performed by those in the church. In fact, it was around the 15th century that it was conclusively proven that the donation never took place. Regardless, Dante feels that Constantine is responsible for corruption in the church.

C ANTO X X

1   Now I will write new lines of new punishments for the
       twentieth canto of this first canticle, the canticle of the submerged.

4   Already I was looking below into the depths, where tears of
       sorrow wet the ground,

7   and I saw in the circle, souls walking, weeping and saying not
       a word, moving slowly like religious processions in our world.

10   As I leaned forward more, I saw, shockingly, that each was
       disfigured between the chin and the chest,

13   so that their faces were twisted to their backs, and walked
       backwards, because they could not see ahead of them.

16   Maybe palsy has distorted some this fully, but I have never
       seen that, and I do not think it possible.

19   So now, reader, may God let you understand what you read;
       now wonder how I could ever keep myself from crying

22   when I saw men's faces twisted, with tears bathing the
       buttocks and dripping down the butt crack.

25   Certainly I wept as I leaned against a rock on that bridge, so
       my guide asked me, "Are you quite as foolish as everyone else?

In this place, only dead pity lives: for is there anyone more   28
evil than he who brings passion to God's Justice?

Raise your head and see the one for whom the earth split   31
open while Thebans watched and cried, 'Amphiaraus, where do
you run?

Have you surrendered?' But he did not hesitate in his fall to   34
Minos, who controls all sinners eventually.

See how his chest has become his shoulders; because he   37
wished to see ahead, he must look behind and walk that way.

Also see Tiresias, who changed his appearance when he   40
became a woman, so changing all his body;

to change back, he had to strike again with his wand two   43
coiled snakes.

And Arruns is he who has his back to Tiresias' belly; Arruns,   46
who lives below in the hills of Luni, where the Carrarese work
the ground,

made his home, a cave of white marble, from which he saw   49
the stars and sea clearly.

And she, who hides her breasts with her disheveled hair,   52
who keeps her hairy parts to the far side,

was Manto, who wandered through many lands and settled   55
in the place where I was born; hear me awhile about this.

When her father died, and the city of Bacchus was enslaved,   58
she wandered many years.

In Italy, between the Alps that enclose Germany above   61
Tirolo, is a lake called Benaco.

64 I think at least a thousand rivers, if not more, must go out of that lake and bathe Pennino, Garda, and Val Camonica.

67 In the middle there is a place that I figure the bishops of Verona, Brescia, and Trento would bless if they came upon it.

70 Peschiera, a strong and beautiful fortress, which was built to face the Brescians and Bergamasques, was built at the lowest part of the shore.

73 In that place falls all the water not held by Benaco, and forms a river.

76 As soon as it forms, it is called the Mincio; it is not called the Benaco until it reaches Governolo, where it meets with the Po.

79 Not far along, it runs through a flat land, and forms a marsh, which is often terribly humid in summer.

82 When she went that way, that savage virgin, she saw a land in the middle, untilled and without inhabitant.

85 There, to avoid human contact, she stayed with her slaves to do her work, there she lived and died, and is buried.

88 Afterward, the people that lived in that area began to meet there, for the marsh surrounding it made a good defense.

91 Over her bones they built a city, and named it Mantua, by mutual agreement, after her name, for she first chose it.

94 Before, far more people lived there, before Casalodi and his foolishness was tricked by Pinamonte.

97 So now, if you ever hear a story of the history of my town contrary to mine, do not be deceived."

And I said, "Master, your words have convinced me; I trust   100
you so that any other person's words would be as useless as used
coals.

But tell me if there are any other spirits worth noticing, for   103
that is all I am wondering."

And he said to me, "That spirit with his beard down his   106
cheeks and his shoulders, when Greece had so few men

that even cradles held few sons, he was a fortune teller. At   109
Aulis, he and Calchas decided when to cut the cables.

His name is Eurypylus; in fact, a part of my high tragedy   112
speaks of him; if you know that part, then you know the entire
story.

That other one, very skinny, was Michael Scot, who knew   115
very well how to play the game of magical deceit.

See also Guido Bonatti; see Asdente, who now wishes that he   118
had not abandoned his cord and leather, but indeed, he repents
too late.

See the women saddened for leaving their sewing needles   121
and tools to become witches; they cast spells with plants and
effigies.

Let us go now, though. Cain with his thorns already is at the   124
border of the hemispheres and touches the sea below Seville.

The moon was full last night, you should know this, for often   127
it was good for you in the dark wood."

This is what he said to me; in the meantime, we walked on.   130

Canto XX Notes

Dante and Virgil, now at the peak of the bridge over the fourth ditch, find the diviners, whose heads are turned backwards. Virgil points out several of them: Amphiaraus, Tiresias, Arruns, and Manto. He then provides a summary of the founding of Mantua, his hometown, by Manto. Having been asked whether any more of the sinners are worthy of notice, Virgil also points out Eurypylus, Michael Scot, Guido Bonatti, and Benvenuto.

1-130. THE DIVINERS: Diviners are all those who attempted to determine the future, an ability reserved only for God. Because they attempted to see forward while on earth, in Hell, their heads are twisted to face backward, and they walk backward, now able only to see what is behind them.

16. palsy: Any of a group of diseases that cause paralysis and contortions of the body.

28-30. pity...passion: The exact meaning of the passion is disputed. What is agreed upon is that Virgil makes it clear that it is not appropriate to pity those in Hell, who cannot be saved.

31-33: Thebans...Amphiaraus: Through a complex series of events, Amphiaraus was convinced by his wife to join a siege on Thebes. Having foreseen his death, he attempted to hide; his wife betrayed his hiding spot, and a thunderbolt from Zeus caused an earthquake that swallowed him up.

35. Minos: The beast in Hell, who sends each sinner to their place, mentioned in Canto 5.

40-45. Tiresias...coiled snakes: According to the version of the legend that Dante would have likely known, Tiresias found two coiled snakes and separated them with a stick (which Dante calls a wand). This action caused him to transform into a woman, until seven years later when he found the same snakes; separating them again, he was turned back into a man. Jupiter (Zeus) and Juno (Hera), arguing over whether the man or woman found more pleasure in sex, asked Tiresias. Tiresias, agreeing with Jupiter, said that it was more pleasurable for a woman; angered by this, Juno caused him to go blind. Jupiter, however, gave him the gift of prophecy, and a life seven times longer.

46-51. Arruns...Luni...Carrarese: Arruns was an Etruscan diviner; Dante describes him as living in a cave in the town of Luni, near Carrara, a place well-known for its white marble. He did not, in fact, live in a cave, nor did he determine the future from stargazing, as Dante suggests.

55. Manto: The daughter of Tiresias. In a strange contradiction, Manto is later stated (in *Purgatorio,* indirectly) as being in Purgatory. Interestingly, Dante as the author has Virgil explain the founding of Mantua in a matter completely different than the explanation which Virgil himself gave in the *Aeneid.*

58. city of Bacchus: Thebes, the birthplace of Bacchus, also called Dionysus, the god of wine.

62-63. Tirolo...Benaco: Benaco is a lake near the vicinity of Tirolo, which borders Austria.

65-66. Pennino, Garda, and Val Camonica: Pennino is a mountain, Garda a commune, and Val Camonica a valley. The Benaco is known as the Garda in modern times.

67-69. bishops of Verona, Brescia, and Trento: In the middle of the lake there is an island. Verona, Brescia, and Trento surround the lake.

70-72. Peschiera...Brescians...Bergamasques: Brescia and Bergamo were cities near the fortress.

76-78. Mincio...Governolo...Po: This river, called the Mincio, travels south to Governolo, and then east, until it flows into the Po.

94-98. Casalodi...Pinamonte: Alberto di Casalodi, who ruled in Mantua, was convinced by Pinamonte, a citizen of Mantua, to banish the unpopular members of the ruling party. After doing so, Pinamonte was able to lead a revolt and regain control of Mantua.

108. so few men: During the Trojan War.

110-112. Aulis...Calchas...Eurypylus: According to Dante, both Eurypylus and Calchas determined when the Trojan fleet should leave the port of Aulis. Actually, according to the *Aeneid,* which is Virgil's 'high tragedy,' only Calchas was responsible for this decision. Again Dante as the author has Virgil contradict the *Aeneid.*

115. Michael Scot: He was a well-known astrologer and alchemist who died in the early 1200s. He is not, however, mentioned among the alchemists in the tenth bolgia.

118. Guido Bonatti: An astrologer.

119. Asdente: A nickname, meaning 'toothless,' for Mastro Benvenuto, a shoemaker turned astrologer.

124-126. Cain...Seville: In old tradition, what is now called 'the man in the moon' was seen as Cain carrying thorns. Therefore, this reference is to the moon setting over the ocean past Seville. It is now early morning on Saturday.

C A N T O X X I

1   We went from that bridge to the next, talking about things which my Comedy will not address. We went to the summit of the next bridge,

4   and stopped to view the next ridge of Malebolge and hear more useless cries. It was incredibly dark!

7   Just as in the winter the Venetians boil a sticky pitch to fix their damaged ships,

10   unfit for sailing, (so some sailors, instead of sailing, build new keels; some fix holes in the boats, damaged from too much travel;

13   some hammer at the prow and others at the stern; some make oars, and some ropes and cords; one will mend the jib and the other the sails),

16   so, not by a fire but by God's will, there was boiling a thick mass of tar that covered the sides of the ditch.

19   I could see it, but not in it; nothing could be seen but bubbles; the rising up and settling of the pitch.

22   And while I watched it eagerly, my master shouted out, "Be careful, be careful!" And he pulled me back from where I was standing.

I turned around like one anxious to see what he ought to be   25
careful of, but then is terrified,

so he continues to run away but still looks back. And so I saw   28
a black demon running across the ridge.

How hideous he seemed, how deliberate his movements!   31

His wings were spread wide and his feet were very quick; he   34
had placed a sinner across his sharp, high shoulders; the sinner
was held with his head down over the demon's back, and the
demon was holding on to his ankles.

On our bridge he yelled out, "Malebranche, I have an elder   37
from Saint Vita for you! Push him under and I'll get some more

from his city; they have so many like him! Bonturo is the   40
only one there that's not a grafter! For money, they'll make any
'no' into a 'yes!'"

Then he tossed the sinner down and ran back across the   43
ridge; indeed, no guard dog has ever run so fast to catch a thief
as he did!

The sinner went under, and rose up again, covered in pitch.   46
The demons, underneath the bridge, shouted, "The Sacred Face
should not be shown here;

in this place, we do not swim like they do in the Serchio; if   49
you want to avoid our hooks, then don't lift your head above the
pitch!"

And they stuck him with a hundred hooks and mocked him: 52
"Here you must dance undercover, and attempt your grabbing in
secret!"

The demons acted just like a cook who has his helpers push   55
meat under with a hook to prevent it from floating.

58   So my good master said to me, "Do not let them see you; hide behind a rock.

61   No matter how they taunt me, don't worry; I know how things work down here; I've seen all these games before."

64   After he said this, he moved past the bridge to the sixth ridge, and there he had to demonstrate his strong will.

67   With the same fervor as dogs have when they come to attack a wretch, who then stops as if to beg to them,

70   so those demons hurried from under the bridge with their hooks, but he yelled, "Can't you be civil for a while?

73   Before you try to hook me, let one of your group come forward. Hear what I have to say, and then decide whether I should be hooked."

76   Hearing this, they barked, "Have Malacoda go!" One moved forward, while the others stayed. He asked them as he came forward, "How can he win?"

79   But my master already responded, "Malacoda, do you really think I've come, as you can see, completely armed against all your traps,

82   without the very will of God and of fate? Let us go on; Heaven wills that I should show this path to another man."

85   Hearing this, Malacoda's pride left him, and he dropped his hooks to his feet. He told his group, "Since that is how things are, we cannot harm him."

88   My guide said to me, "You who are crouching, low among the broken rocks of the bridge, you are now safe; return to me."

So I got up quickly and moved to where he was. All the demons inched toward me; I feared they had forgotten their promise! 91

Just so, I saw how when the infantry marched out under guard from Caprona, they shook as they passed their enemies. 94

I moved closer to my guide, while constantly watching the demons, for they cast me less than kind looks. 97

They were bending their hooks and shouting, "Shall I stick him in the rump?" And they all shouted back, "Yes! Give it to him!" 100

Malacoda, who was still talking to my good guide, quickly turned to them and said, "Shut up, Scarmiglione!" 103

He said to us, "There is no use going farther on this ridge, as the sixth bridge is smashed at the bottom of the ditch. 106

But if you still go ahead, walk along the edge of the ridge; nearby there is a bridge intact. 109

Yesterday, five hours from now, one thousand, two hundred sixty-six years had passed since the bridge was destroyed. 112

I'm already sending ten of my group that way to see if any sinner dares to stick his head up for air; you can go with them, for they have no evil intentions. 115

Now, come forward, Alichino and Calcabrina, Cagnazzo; Barbariccia, you can head this ten. 118

Libicocco, go, and Draghignazzo, and Ciriatto with the tusks, and Graffiacane and Fargello, and furious Rubicante. 121

Look all around in the pitch; and keep these two safe until you reach the next bridge that goes intact across the ditch." 124

127   "Ah, me! What is happening, master?" I said, "Can't we go alone? If you know the way, I want no one else along.

130   If you are as smart as always, can you not see how the demons are grinding their teeth? I can see the promise of trouble in their faces!"

133   And he responded, "I don't want you to be afraid; let them gnash their teeth away; they do it for the sinners in the pitch."

136   They turned around to the left of the bank: First, each signaled their leader, Barbariccia, by sticking out their tongue towards him.

139   And he farted, making his ass a trumpet.

Canto XXI Notes

Progressing to the top of the bridge over the fifth ditch, Dante sees that it is filled with a boiling tar. After seeing a demon toss a sinner into the pitch, Virgil and Dante meet the Malebranche, a group of demons that guard the fifth bolgia, where barraters are kept. Malacoda, the leader of the demons, sends ten to escort Dante and Virgil to the next ditch.

1-139. THE BARRATERS: In the fifth ditch, barraters, those who used political offices and power for personal gain, are found (in modern times, 'grafters' is the preferred term). Various barraters will be mentioned in Canto 22. Barraters are punished by being submerged in boiling tar. If they rise above the surface to relieve some of the pain, but are spotted, they are hooked by the Malebranche.

37. Malebranche: Meaning 'evil claws.' They are a band of demons who use hooks to torture the barraters.

38. Saint Zita: Zita is a saint whose bodies remains in the city of Lucca. The elders of Lucca were the officials of the city.

40. Bonturo: Bonturo Dati; the statement is an irony, as he was one of the worst of the grafters in Lucca.

48. Sacred Face: This was a wooden figure of Christ that was honored in Lucca. Most scholars believe either that the reference is made by the demons because the sinner, now coated in black tar, resembles the wooden figure, or else, if the sinner has lifted his back up above the pitch, that he would appear to be bowing like one would in front of the Sacred Face.

49. Serchio: A river near Lucca, popular for swimming.

76. Malacoda: Meaning 'evil tail'; he is the apparent leader of the Malebranche.

95. Caprona: When the Tuscans attacked Caprona in 1289, those from Caprona were promised safe passage out if they surrendered. Dante now relates to their uneasiness in the presence of their enemies.

112-114. Yesterday...five hours...years ago: At the time of the death of Christ, which caused the great earthquake in Hell. Many ancient sources would place the time of Christ's death at noon, whereas the Bible places it at 3 p.m. Therefore, it is now either 7 or 10 a.m. on Saturday.

CANTO XXII

1   I have seen horseman start a march and attack, and at times retreat;

4   and in the land of the Aretines, I've seen archers and raiding parties gallop; I've seen jousts in tournaments,

7   done with trumpets, or bells, or drums, with signs from castles, with native instruments and foreign ones;

10   but I have never seen horsemen, or infantry, or ships that sail by so strange a trumpet!

13   We went along with that company of ten demons; what a furious group! Yet, as they say, "in taverns with drunks."

16   I watched the pitch attentively, to see all I could about the sinners and the place where they burned.

19   Just as dolphins with arched backs signal sailors that a storm is coming, so that they may save their ship,

22   so every once in a while, a sinner would show his back above the pitch to relieve his pain a little, and then hide again, faster than lightning.

25   Just as frogs crouch on the edge of a ditch, with only their noses above the water line, to hide their feet and bodies,

so the sinners crouched in this place; faster than a flash, they   28
dove under when Barbariccia came near.

I still shudder to remember one sinner who was too slow, just   31
as a frog may be left behind when the others dive below;

Graffiacane, who was nearest to that sinner, hooked him by   34
his messy hair and pulled him up, looking like an otter.

By this time, I knew all the names of the demons, for I was   37
listening when they had been chosen, and watched as they had
stepped forward.

"Rubicante, set your talons right into him, to tear his skin!"   40
So all those cursed demons yelled out together.

And I said, "My master, if you are able, find out the name of   43
that man who has become a victim."

My guide went over to the sinner, and asked him his   46
birthplace. He answered, "I come from the kingdom of Navarre.

My mother, who conceived me with a vagabond, a destroyer   49
of his property and his body, put me into the service of a lord.

Then I went into the house of the worthy King Thibault,   52
there I started to steal; I pay for that sin with this heat."

Ciriatto, who had two tusks coming from his mouth like a   55
hog, let that sinner feel how they could rip.

The mouse had come into the company of evil cats; but   58
Barbariccia came and held his arm, saying, "Stand away, while
I hook him!"

And turning to my master he said, "Ask more questions, if   61
you want to know more before the others finish him."

64   So my guide said, "Now tell us, are there any Italians among
these sinners?" And he said, "I just left one

67   who was nearby; I wish I were hidden like him, for then I
would have no fear of hooks and tusks!"

70   Libicocco said, "We've wasted enough time already!" and
taking his hook, ripped out a chunk of flesh from an arm.

73   Draghignazzo looked like he wanted to grab his legs, so their
leader turned and threatened them all with his stare.

76   After they'd settled down some, my guide quickly asked the
sinner, who was staring at his wound,

79   "Who was that one you left to come here unluckily, as you
said just before?" He replied, "Fra Gomita

82   of Gallura, who was capable of every type of fraud. He held
his master's enemies, but dealt in a way that pleased all of them.

85   He took their money and let them go, as he explains himself;
he was a clever, not a common, deceiver.

88   His friend there is Don Michele Zanche from Logodoro; they
talk constantly of Sardinia.

91   Ah! See that one there grinding his teeth! I would say more if
I were not so afraid; he is preparing to hook me!"

94   So their great chief, now looking at Farfarello, who rolled
his eyes, being so anxious to attack, said, "Get out of here, you
disgusting bird!"

97   "If you want to hear or see," that scared sinner started,
"Lombards or Tuscans, I can get some for you.

100   But have the Malebranche step away, so that my friends will
not fear them. Standing here,

I can, though alone right now, make seven more show up by   103
whistling, as we always do when one of us can get out."

Hearing that, Cagnazzo lifted his head, shaking it, saying,   106
"Just listen to him and his trick he'll use to escape!"

The sinner, full of tricks, replied, "Then I have too many   109
tricks, if I bring more punishment to my friends!"

Alichino had had enough, and cried out, "If you jump back   112
in, I will not go after you,

but fly above the pitch. We will go hide behind the rocks and   115
see if you can handle us by yourself."

Reader, now you will hear of this odd game: Each of them   118
turned to look across the ditch, indeed, he who was at first the
most unwilling turned first.

The Navarrese, picking his time carefully, had prepared to   121
jump, and then instantly launched himself and was free of their
leader.

Now all the demons felt guilty, especially the demon that   124
was at fault; so he flew off, yelling, "You will be caught!"

But this was no use, for his wings were not faster than fear;   127
the sinner went right under the pitch, and the demon, flying back
up by lifting his chest,

just as the falcon does when a wild duck escapes him, diving   130
and then flying back upset.

Calcabrina, angered by this trick, flew towards Alichino. He   133
was happy that the sinner was freed, for he had been hoping for
a fight.

As soon as the Navarrese was gone, he turned his talons upon   136
the other demon, and they brawled over the ditch.

139 But Alichino fought well, for he was indeed like a full-grown hawk; so both fell into the boiling pond.

142 Indeed, the heat was quick to separate them, but they could not get out, for their wings were coated in the gluey pitch.

145 Barbariccia, saddened with the test, sent four out to the other bank with their hooks, and quickly

148 they took their positions, and they sent their hooks to those two, already cooked in the pitch.

151 And we left them alone to sort out that mess.

Canto XXII Notes

Led by the Malebranche, Dante and Virgil cross over the fifth bridge. They find a sinner, who, unable to hide himself in time, is hooked by the demons. He mentions two other barraters, and claims that he can lure more out of the pitch by whistling, if the Malebranche hide. They do so, and the sinner jumps back in the pitch. The demons begin fighting among themselves, and Dante and Virgil move on without them.

4. Arentines: This likely refers to the battle of Campaldino, in which Dante took part.

48-54. Navarre...Thibault: Early commentators give the sinner the name Ciampolo, though nothing is known of him besides what is stated here: He is from Navarre, a region in northern Spain, and practiced barratry while in the service of king Theobald II of Navarre.

81-84. Fra Gomita of Gallura: He was in charge of prisoners in Gallura, the northeastern part of Sardinia, an island off the coast of Italy; he accepted bribes to let them free.

88-89. Don Michel Zanche from Logodoro: An official in Sardinia; after the king of Sardinia left and never returned, Zanche married the queen and ruled Sardinia until his death.

CANTO XXIII

1   Silent, with no one leading us, we went on with one in front, one following, as minor friars do in procession.

4   That scuffle reminded me of Aesop's fable of the mouse and the frog, for

7   'mo' and 'issa' are no more the same than that story and this event, if you carefully compare their beginnings and ends.

10   And just as one thought comes from another, another thought came from that one, which only increased my fear.

13   I thought: "They have been shamed due to us, and that event caused so much pain and scorn that they surely hate us now!

16   If their anger is added to their malice, they'll chase us more furiously than a dog that's trapped a rabbit."

19   I could feel my hair curling up in fear, and I watched behind me closely while I said, "Master, if you don't hide

22   us now, the Malebranche frightens me, for they are coming for us; I can imagine their sound now!"

25   He responded, "Even if I were a mirror, I would not reflect your outer image faster than your inner.

Now our thoughts are the same; both our actions and ideas   28
are the same, for we have come to the same conclusion.

If the ledge on our right is not too steep, we can go down into   31
the next ditch and hide from their imaginary pursuit."

Even before he finished explaining his plan, I saw them   34
coming towards us with wings stretched out, very much intent
on capturing us.

My guide picked me up in an instant, just as a mother would,   37
waking from a loud noise and seeing a blazing fire,

snatch her son and run without stopping, for she cares more   40
for that son than even for her own life, and so she does not even
pause to put on clothing;

so down the rocky ledge he laid on his back and slid down.   43

Even water does not run so quickly to turn a waterwheel,   46
even when it is near the paddles,

as my master rushed down that ledge, holding me to his   49
chest, like I was a son and not a companion.

Even before we reached the bottom of that ditch, the ten   52
demons were over the edge; but we had nothing to fear,

because High Providence had assigned them to preside over   55
the fifth ditch, so they cannot ever leave it.

Here we saw painted men, walking slowly in circles, and   58
crying, who had looks of weariness and defeat in their faces.

They had cloaks with hoods that covered their eyes,   61
somewhat like the cloaks made for the monks at Cluny.

64   On the outside, their cloaks shone, for they were trimmed with gold, but on the inside they were made of lead, and so heavy that Frederick's were like straw in comparison.

67   Oh, what a heavy cloak for all eternity! Once more we turned left and watched their cries,

70   but because the weight of the cloak was so great, they moved so slow that with every step we had another man standing next to us.

73   I said to my guide, "Please find someone whom I would know by name or action, watching them as we walk."

76   One, who understood my Tuscan dialect, behind us, yelled out, "Stop your walking, you who are running in the dark air!

79   Perhaps I can tell you what you want!" So my leader stopped and said, "Wait for awhile, and then walk at his speed."

82   I stood still and I saw two men with faces that showed their desire to catch up with me, but their great burden and the great crowd slowed them.

85   When they finally reached me, they looked at me for a while with a scrutinizing eye, and they said nothing until they faced each other and said,

88   "The movement of his throat makes him seem alive...but if he is dead, what right do they have to come here without a heavy mantle?"

91   Then they said to me, "Tuscan, you who have joined this group of sad hypocrites, do not refrain from sharing your name."

94   I said, "I was born and raised in that place where the river Arno is, in the great city, and I have the body I've always had.

Who are you, whose tears come from all your pain? What is   97
this punishment that sparkles so?"

One of them said, "These orange robes are so heavy with lead   100
that they make our bones creak.

We were Jolly Friars, from Bologna. My name was Catalano,   103
and his was Loderingo, and we were both appointed by your city

to keep the peace, even though it is traditional to choose only   106
one. And by the state of things around the Gardingo, you can still
know that we had that position."

I started, "O Friars, your evil..." but I said nothing else, for I   109
saw a man crucified onto the ground by three nails.

When he saw me, he writhed on the ground, breathing   112
heavily into his beard. Brother Catalano, who noticed,

said, "That man staked there, at whom you are staring, told   115
the Pharisees that it would be good for the people to put a certain
man to death.

He lies naked in the road, as you can see, so that if anyone   118
passes him on the road, he feels their weight.

His father-in-law, and also all the council that did such bad   121
things for the Jews, are all punished in the same way here."

I saw Virgil fascinated at this man, punished in such a   124
demeaning manner for eternity.

He said to the friar, "If you are so allowed, please tell us if   127
there is some slope on the right

by which we can climb out of here, without needing the   130
black angels to come down and carry us." And he said,

133 "Even sooner than you hope, we are coming upon a bridge that crosses all these valleys,

136 except, it is broken over this one. You can climb up the rubble, which slopes up the side and is heaped at the bottom."

139 My leader stood looking down for a while, and said, "He who hooks sinners on this side will angrily remember these events."

142 And the friar said, "While in Bologna, I once heard of many different sins of the devil, among them, that he is a liar, and the father of lies."

145 So my leader walked with great steps, his face somewhat contorted with anger; so I left those ones with the burden,

148 and walked in the prints of his dear feet.

Canto XXIII Notes

Dante and Virgil go on without the demons, fearing that they will chase them. Seeing them approach, Dante and Virgil slide down into the sixth ditch, where they find the hypocrites. They speak with Catalano, who mentions Loderingo, and also points out Caiaphas, who is crucified to the ground. He also indicates when they are approaching a bridge over the sixth ditch, but it is broken, revealing that Malacoda lied to Virgil about the bridge still standing.

4-9. 'mo'... 'issa'...Aesop's fable: 'Mo' and 'issa' are both words meaning 'now': Dante compares the events of the demons with a story of Aesop in which a frog deceives a mouse wishing to cross a river: They tie a cord between them so the mouse will not fall off, but the frog dives down and begins to drown the mouse; a hawk, seeing the mouse, picks him up, and the frog is carried with. Assuming Dante refers to the version in which the mouse escapes, the mouse represents the Navarrese sinner, the frog is Alichino, and the hawk is Calcabrina.

58-148. THE HYPOCRITES: Hypocrites are punished by wearing beautiful, gilded cloaks, which are in fact incredible heavy, as they are made of lead; they are forced to circle eternally. One sinner, Caiaphas, is crucified to the ground, where all the hypocrites must walk on top of him.

63: Cluny: The cloaks for the monks at Cluny, in France, were especially nice.

66. Frederick's: According to a tradition at that time, Frederick II executed traitors by cloaking them in lead and placing them in a heated cauldron, causing the lead to melt around them.

95. great city: This city is Florence.

103. Jolly Friars: The Jolly Friars were an order of friars dedicated to keeping peace; however, their corruption and disregard for their own rules earned them a bad reputation.

103-108. Catalano...Loderingo...Gardingo: Catalano was a Guelf and Loderingo a Ghibelline; they were appointed as peacekeepers in Florence in hopes that their opposing viewpoints would help them mediate tensions between the Guelfs and Ghibellines (though members of the order were forbidden to accept political office). However, Dante apparently felt that they did nothing to stop violence in Gardingo, which resulted in the destruction of the homes of the Uberti family, who were prominent Ghibellines.

115-123. that man...father-in-law...council: This is the high priest Caiaphas; fearing Jesus as a threat, he suggested that Jesus be killed rather than allowing all the Jewish nation to die. His father-in-law is Annas, who presided over the Sanhedrin, the council that condemned Jesus. The rest of the Pharisees are also crucified on the ground.

Canto XXIV

1   In that part of the young year when the sun is under Aquarius and the nights begin to move south,

4   when the frost of the ground mimics her white sister, but only for a short while,

7   a peasant, running short on food, gets up to look at his fields, and finds them white; so he strikes his hip in anger,

10   and goes about complaining like a clueless wretch; then he goes out again and puts hope in his basket,

13   seeing that the ground has changed quickly; and he takes his staff and takes his sheep to feed;

16   so my master frightened me when he had had a look of confusion, but he quickly applied a bandage to that wound,

19   because when we arrived at the fallen bridge I saw once again the good face I saw first at the mountain.

22   Having first observed the wreck carefully, he picked me up once again.

25   And like one who judges each action and looks ahead, just so, as he carried me up the rocks

he would look to the next and say, "Go to that one next; first, 28
see if it will support you."

The journey was not at all fit for someone with a cloak, for 31
even though he was light and I was being helped, it was still a
difficult path for us.

If it were not that this wall was shorter than the one on 34
the other side, I would not have been able to climb it, though I
cannot speak for him.

But, because Malebolge is constantly sloping down towards 37
the lowest pit, it is required

that each pit have one tall and one short wall. Finally, we 40
reached the last rock that was broken off.

I was so out of breath when we got there that I sat down 43
right away.

"From this point on, you must put off your laziness," my 46
master said, "for men do not find fame while on cushions or
under bed sheets;

and anyone who lives his life fameless leaves his legacy like 49
smoke in the air or foam on water.

So stand up, and overcome your weakness with the spirit 52
that overcomes in all battles, if the heavy body does not crush it.

We must still go a harder way; it is not enough that we have 55
left them behind us; if you understand what I'm saying, benefit
from it."

So I got up with more breath than before and said to him, 58
"Let's go, for I am stronger and more prepared!"

We went up onto the bridge, which had much more ragged 61
and difficult boulders, and was more steeply sloped.

64   Not to seem weak, I spoke as we went on; because of this, a voice came from below us in the ditch, sounding like a voice not fit to speak.

67   I don't know what his words were, though even then I was in the middle of the ditch; yet, I think he was moving.

70   I leaned over, but my mortal eyes could not see to the bottom through the dark; I said, "Master, when you come

73   to the next bridge, can we go into this next ditch? I hear a voice, but cannot understand it, and can make out nothing when I look down, so let us descend the wall."

76   "The only way I can respond is by doing so," he said. "A reasonable request ought to be answered by the action, not words."

79   So we climbed down the bridge at the end where it meets the eighth ridge, and then I could see the ditch clearly;

82   I saw a terrifying mass of snakes, so frightening that remembering them still makes me pale.

85   Libya cannot brag about her desert, for her Chelydri, Jaculi, and Cenchres, which she mates with Amphisbaena and Phareae,

88   were never so numerous in all of Ethiopia or all the coast of the Red Sea, as the number of plagues and punishments here!

91   In this horrid group, people ran, naked and terrified, without hope of a hole or a heliotrope stone.

94   The snakes tied their hands behind their backs; they had curled themselves around their legs and were knotted.

97   Just there! a snake darted up at a man near us, and bit him where the neck meets the shoulder.

No 'O' or 'I' has ever been written faster than that soul burst   100
into flames, and falling, turned to ashes.

Where he lay on the ground, his dust grouped once again and   103
formed what it had been before,

just as, so wise men say, a phoenix will die and be born again   106
near its five-hundredth birthday;

its entire life, it never eats grass or grains, but only incense   109
and amomum, and nard and myrrh.

Like one who falls suddenly, not knowing whether it is some   112
demon dragging him down, or some other force that controls
men,

who looks around when he gets back up, confused by the   115
great anguish, and sighs over it,

so this sinner stared at us when he got up. Oh, how great is   118
God's power when it brings forth such punishments!

My guide asked him who he was, and he said, "I fell from   121
Tuscany into this pit not long ago.

I lived a bestial life, not a good human one, for mule I was; I   124
am Vanni Fucci, the beast; Pistoia was a good den for me."

I said to my guide, "Tell him to not sneak away, and ask him   127
what his sin was that brought him here; when I saw him, he was
a bloody, violent man."

The sinner, who heard me, did not pretend that he had not,   130
and so turned his face and mind to me, with a look of great shame.

He said, "I feel greater pain now in you catching me here in   133
this state than I did when I was taken from my life.

136 I will not refuse your request: I am here because I stole sacred relics from the sacred place,

139 and another was held responsible. Unless you find happiness in seeing me here, if you ever leave this dark place,

142 listen to my message. Pistoia will lose its Blacks, and Florence will gain a new people, and new laws.

145 Mars is bringing out a hot wind wrapped in clouds from Val di Magra, and those people will fight with great bitterness and violence

148 above Campo Piceno; and he will break up the cloud and all the Whites will be killed by it.

151 I tell you this so you may grieve over it!"

CANTO XXIV NOTES

Dante and Virgil leave the sixth bolgia by climbing up the rubble of the ruined bridge. From there they walk onto the bridge over the seventh ditch, where thieves are held; Dante hears a voice, but cannot make out what it is saying, or where in the ditch it is coming from, so they follow the bridge to the end, where they stand on the ridge and can see clearly into the ditch, which is filled with snakes. Dante observes the sinner Vanni Fucci, who is bit by a snake, bursts into flames, and reforms from his ashes. Fucci makes a prophecy concerning the Guelphs.

1-3. Aquarius: That is, from January 21 to February 21.

4-15. frost...white sister: The peasant wakes to find frost on the ground; thinking it is snow, he fears he has lost his crops; when the frost melts, he is relieved.

31-32. a cloak: A reference to the cloaks of the hypocrites in Canto 23, which are made of lead.

64-151. THE THIEVES: Thieves are punished in the seventh bolgia, which is addressed in Cantos 24-26. The ditch is filled with snakes and reptiles that constantly steal and exchange forms with the sinners in striking transformations.

85-90. Libya...Ethiopia...Red Sea: All these are kinds of serpents mentioned in Lucan's *Pharsalia* as being found in the regions of Libya, Ethiopia, and the Red Sea.

110-111. incense...amomum...nard...myrrh: All are expensive spices; tradition held that the phoenix built its nest of spices, which caught fire from the heat of the sun.

124-126. Vanni Fucci...Pistoia: Vanni Fucci was an illegitimate child; some early commentators remark that his nickname was 'Vanni the Beast.' He was born in Pistoia, where the split between the White and Black Guelfs originated.

137-139. sacred relics...other: Vanni Fucci and two others stole from the chapel of St. James, and an innocent man was charged with the crime; however, the truth eventually was found out when one of Fucci's accomplices confessed. By this time, however, Fucci had fled Pistoia.

142-150. Blacks...Campo Piceno: Fucci prophesies the Whites driving out the Blacks in Pistoia in 1301, which was followed in 1302 by the Blacks retaliating at Piceno. The reference to the 'hot wind' is interpreted by some as being a person (Moroello Malaspina) who would aid the Blacks, and by others as a kind of meteorological analogy for the Blacks and Whites colliding like a hot wind and mist.

Canto XXV

1   When he had finished speaking, that thief raised up his hands and made them into figs, yelling, "Have these, God, I've made them just for you!"

4   From that point on, the snakes were my friends, for one wrapped around his neck as if to say, "I will let him speak no longer!"

7   Another wrapped his arms, and tied them together so tight he could make no movement at all.

10   Pistoia, Pistoia, why do you not just destroy yourself, for you do more evil than your children?

13   In all the dark circles of Hell, I saw no sinner stand so firmly against God, not even he who fell off the wall at Thebes.

16   He ran without saying anything more; I saw a furious centaur crying, "Where is that evil one?"

19   I do not think even Maremma has as many snakes as that centaur had on his back.

22   A dragon spreading his wings is between his shoulders, and sets aflame any person they encounter.

25   My master told me, "He is Cacus, who made lakes of blood many times under the rocks of Mount Aventine.

He does not take the same profession as his brothers, because   28
he stole by fraud a great herd of sheep he found;

so his cross-eyed actions ended under the club of Hercules,   31
which gave him a hundred blows, though he did not feel ten of
them."

While talking, that centaur passed under us, and three more   34
spirits appeared, though we did not notice them

until they said, "Who are you?" So, we stopped our talking,   37
and they caught our attention.

I did not recognize them, but it so happened, as it will by   40
chance sometimes, that one of them gave the name of another,

and said, "Where did Cianfa go?" I, so that my leader should   43
listen, put my finger over my lips to signal silence.

If you do not believe what I am saying, reader, I am not   46
surprised, for I saw it, and hardly believe it myself!

As I was watching them, a six-legged serpent wrapped itself   49
around one of them.

Its middle feet wrapped up his waist, and its front feet   52
wrapped his arms; then it bit his cheeks with its fangs;

its back feet covered his legs, and it put its tail between them,   55
and wrapped it up his back.

Ivy has never wrapped a tree as quickly as that creature   58
wrapped around his limbs.

Once they had begun to stick to each other like hot wax, and   61
mixed their colors, neither appeared the same,

just like paper burning, where a brown color comes before   64
the flame; not yet black, but no longer white.

67   The other two stared at him, and cried, "Oh, Agnel, you are changing! Already, you are neither two nor one."

70   The two heads were now one, so that the appearances of both were now mixed, and the two heads were lost.

73   The arms became two from the four; the thighs and legs, and the belly and chest became like something never seen before.

76   All the prior appearances were destroyed; the disgusting figure was both two and neither, and it slowly walked forward.

79   As a lizard, moving from one hiding spot to another in the heat of dog-days, crosses the road like a flash of lightning,

82   so a small serpent seemed, black like the color of pepper, as it came towards those other two,

85   and it pierced into one of them in the stomach, and then fell to the ground in front of him.

88   He watched the serpent, but said nothing; rather, he yawned, as if from tiredness or fever.

91   He stared at the serpent, and the serpent back at him; he through his wound, and it through its mouth were smoking, and the smoke from each combined.

94   Let Lucan say nothing of Sabellus and Nasidius, and let him listen.

97   Let Ovid say nothing about Cadmus and Arethusa, for if he makes him into a serpent, and her a fountain, in his poetry, I am not jealous,

100   for he never had two different things exchange their substance.

The man and serpent answered each other as they were able: 103
the serpent's tail split in half, and the wounded sinner brought
his feet together.

His legs joined together, and soon no mark was left to indicate   106
a joining between them.

The split tail began to take the shape the sinner was losing; its   109
skin softened, but his skin hardened.

I saw that his arms shrunk into his armpits; the beasts' two   112
feet were lengthening as his were shortening.

Then its hind feet twisted together to form that organ which   115
a man hides, and the sinner's became the two hind feet.

While the smoke was dividing them, it gave them each a new   118
color; on one side, the creature gained hair; on the other side, the
sinner lost his.

One stood up, the other fell on the ground, but they did not   121
look about with their evil lamps, for they were each watching as
their snouts changed.

He who was standing brought his snout in towards his head,   124
and the extra flesh became ears over his tight cheeks;

that flesh which didn't go to the ears became a nose, and the   127
rest filled out the cheeks to the normal size.

He who was lying on the ground, extended his snout out, and   130
his ears withdrew into his head as a snail withdraws its horns.

His tongue, which before was complete, and capable of   133
speech, split, and the other's forked tongue joined together; and
then the smoke stopped.

The soul that became a beast ran hissing in the ditch; the   136
other spit as he chased after him.

139   He turned his new back on the serpent and said to the other man, "I want Buoso to run on all sixes, as I have had to."

142   So I watched the population of this seventh ditch change again and again; if my pen ever fails to record correctly, let the uniqueness of this situation excuse my error.

145   Though my eyes were confused, and my spirit had no power, the souls could not run so quickly

148   that I did not see very clearly Puccio Sciancato; he was the only one of the three companions from before who had not been transformed.

151   The other one was he who makes Gaville weep.

CANTO XXV NOTES

Vanni Fucci makes an obscene gesture toward God, and is overtaken by snakes. Dante observes a centaur, Cacus, and three more spirits, who undergo a series of transformations: Cianfa, already having become a six-legged lizard, combines with Agnel. Another sinner, presumed to be Francesco de' Cavalcanti, also a lizard, bites Buoso; exchanging forms, Francesco becomes a man again, and Buoso a lizard. Dante also finds Puccio Sciancato.

2. figs: An obscene hand gesture, probably the gesture made by placing the thumb between the index and middle fingers.

14-15. he who fell off the wall at Thebes: Capaneus, who was mentioned in Canto 14.

19. Maremma: A swampy region near Tuscany.

25-33. Cacus...Hercules: Cacus was, to begin, not necessarily a centaur in mythology, but was only described as 'half-human.' He lived in a cave under Mount Aventine, and stole Hercules' cattle, for which Hercules beat him to death. Because of this sin, he is condemned to the seventh ditch; all other centaurs guard the Phlegethon.

43-78. Cianfa...Agnel: This is the second of the recorded transformations (Vanni Fucci being the first). The group of three sinners wonder where Cianfa (about whom we know nothing other than his family) has gone; he is in fact, the six-legged serpent who joins with one of the sinners, Agnel, a Ghibelline, about whom little is known for sure.

94-99. Lucan...Ovid: Dante refers to two stories of transformations, and claims that the transformations he witnesses are far more impressive. Lucan records a story of soldiers Sabellus and Nasidius, who were bitten by monsters, causing Sabellus to melt and Nasidius to inflate; Ovid records stories of Cadmus being transformed into a serpent, and Arethusa into a fountain.

140-141. Buoso: The as-of-yet unnamed sinner calls the one with whom he exchanged forms Buoso; the identity of Buoso is not known for certain.

148. Puccio Sciancato: A Ghibelline.

151. the other one: The unidentified sinner is now revealed as Francesco de' Cavalcanti; he was murdered by citizens of Gaville, prompting his family to kill many of the citizens in revenge.

CANTO XXVI

1   Be proud, Florence, you are great, and beat your wings over land and sea, and your name is found all through Hell!

4   In the midst of the thieves I found five of your citizens, and I feel shame; you can have no higher honor than them!

7   But if early-morning dreams become reality, you will feel, not long from now, what Prato, among others, wishes for you;

10 if it had already come, it would not be early. I wish that it had, for it must come eventually! It will become a heavier burden as I grow older.

13 We left that place, and went up the steps of rocks that we had used earlier, my leader ahead of me and bringing me forward.

16 As we went up that lonely way, our feet were not enough without our hands.

19 I grieved then, and now I do again, considering what I saw, and I control my intellect more than usual,

22 so that it does nothing without virtue guiding it; if a good star, or something greater, has given me this good, then I will not forsake it.

25 As many fireflies as the peasant sees in the valley when he works his field,

(while on the hillside in that season when he who lights the   28
world hides his face least of all, and when the fly leaves and the
mosquito comes),

it was with that many lights of flames the eight ditch was   31
shining, so I saw when I could look down into it.

Just as he who avenged himself with bears saw Elijah's   34
chariot going up as the horses went into Heaven,

so that he could not look and see anything more than the   37
flame itself, rising like a cloud,

so each flame moves around the ditch; each flame steals a   40
sinner and hides him, though none of them shows its theft.

I was standing on the bridge to see, and had I not been   43
holding on to a rock, I would have fallen.

My leader, who saw me gazing so intently, said, "In the   46
flames are the spirits; each is covered with what burned inside
him."

"My master," I said, "I am more certain hearing you; but, this   49
has already occurred to me, and I wanted to ask you:

Who is in the flame that is so divided it could have come   52
from the funeral pyre of Eteocles and his brother?"

He answered, "Punished in there is Ulysses and Diomedes;   55
now they are punished together just as they were angry with
each other.

In the flame they cry over the trick of the horse that let the   58
noble people of Rome escape through the gate.

They weep for the same reason that Deidamia, though dead,   61
weeps for Achilles; there, they are punished for the Palladium."

64   "If they are able to speak in the flames," I said, "master, I beg you and beg again, so that each of my prayers is worth a thousand,

67   that you do not refuse to wait until that forked flame comes this way; see how I watch it with desire!"

70   He said to me, "Your prayer is to be praised, so I will grant it; but see that you watch your tongue.

73   Allow me to speak to them, for I know what you want from them; and maybe they would ignore your words, for they were Greek."

76   When the flame came to where my leader considered to be the right time and place, I heard him say this:

79   "You two, in one flame; if I deserved anything from you while I lived, whether much or little,

82   when I wrote my poem, stay here; let one of you tell me where you went to die when you were lost."

85   The larger fork of the old flame began shaking and murmuring, like a fire blown by wind.

88   Then its peak began to move slightly back and forth, like it was a tongue, and a voice said, "When

91   I left Circe, who kept me more than a year near Gaeta, even before Aeneas named it that,

94   neither the goodness of a son, nor compassion for my old father, nor my love for Penelope, which would have cheered her,

97   could defeat the desire I had to experience all the world, and human vices and honor of men.

100   Rather, I set out alone on the open sea, with just one ship and the small group that had not deserted me.

I could see as far as Spain and Morocco, their two shores, and the islands of Sardinia and others in that sea.   103

We were old and slow when we came to that narrow passage which Hercules had marked   106

so that no one would travel it; I had passed Seville on my right, and Ceuta on my left.   109

'Brothers,' I said, 'you who have survived a hundred thousand trials to reach the west, while we still have our senses,   112

let us go and experience by following the sun, the land without people.   115

You are humans: You were not born to be like animals; you were born to seek knowledge and virtue.'   118

I made my companions so keen for voyage with this speech, that after that I could not keep them back.   121

Turning our ship toward the morning, we made our oars like wings of a crazy flight, always moving to the left.   124

I could already see the stars of the south pole, and the stars of our own pole were so low they did not rise above the water.   127

Five times the light of the moon came and left since we went through the pass,   130

when we saw a dark mountain, taller than any I'd seen before.   133

We were cheering, but that quickly became weeping, for a whirlwind came from that mountain and struck our ship.   136

It spun the ship in the water three times, and on the fourth the stern was lifted and the prow sank, so to please another,   139

until the waters came over us."   142

CANTO XXVI NOTES

Dante and Virgil progress from the seventh bolgia to the bridge over the eight; looking in, Dante finds that it is lit by many flames. Each flame contains a spirit of an evil counselor. They go to speak to the flame that holds Ulysses and Diomedes. Ulysses recounts the story of his final voyage and death (which appears to have been almost totally created by Dante as author, apart from the year involving Circe).

7. early-morning dreams: It was common belief at the time that dreams which occurred right before waking foretold the future.

9-12. Prato: In 1304, Cardinal Niccolo da Prato was sent to settle the dispute between the fighting political groups in Florence. No compromise was made, and Prato cursed both parties; not long after, a bridge collapsed, and on a separate occasion, a great fire broke out. Both were blamed on the curse.

19-142. THE EVIL COUNSELORS: Those who gave evil counsel are punished in the eighth bolgia, where they are encased in tongues of flame.

52-54. Eteocles and his brother: Eteocles and Polynices both became rulers of Thebes when their father, Oedipus, died. They agreed to alternate ruling for a year; however, when Eteocles refused to allow Polynices to take the throne, Polynices led a siege on Thebes, which resulted in both of their deaths. They were burned on the same funeral pyre, and it was said that their hatred for each other was so great that the flame split into two separate tongues. The tongue that Dante sees will also contain two men.

55-63. Ulysses and Diomedes: Punished in this single flame is both Ulysses, also called Odysseus, and Diomedes. They are punished for three reasons recorded here: First, for the Trojan horse, which caused the fall of Troy; second, for the death of Deidamia, who was in love with Achilles and died of grief when Ulysses convinced him to go to war; and third, for Ulysses' theft of a bust of Athena from the Palladium, which was believed to hold the power to defeat Troy.

91-96. Circe...Gaeta...Penelope: Circe was a witch who turned many of Ulysses' men into swine. After tricking her, Ulysses successfully freed his men; however, they all stayed on the island for a year, Ulysses delaying the return to his home and wife, Penelope. In this account, Circe's island is located near Gaeta, a coastal area of Italy.

109. which Hercules had marked: This is the Strait of Gibraltar, which passes between Ceuta, in Africa, and Seville (which was a general term for Spain). Hercules had marked it because it was believed that past it was the western edge of the world.

130. Five times: That is, five months.

133. dark mountain: This is the Mountain of Purgatory, which in the Divine Comedy is located in the Southern Hemisphere, directly opposite Hell; this geography will be further discussed in Canto 34.

Canto XXVII

1 Now the flame was standing straight and quiet, not speaking,
and it had left us when my good poet had given it permission.

4 Then another, following it, made us watch its tip, for a
strange sound was coming from it.

7 Just like the Sicilian bull, which first cried out with the cries
of him who formed it with his tools,

10 used to give out the cry of the punished, so that, though it
was made of bronze, it seemed to be in pain;

13 so the words of the flame, having no mouth, became the
language of a fire.

16 But, when they found the tip, they gave the tip the waving
the sinner's tongue had given when it formed the words,

19 and we heard it say, "You, for whom I speak, who were just
discussing Lombard, saying, 'Now you can go, I will keep you no
longer,'

22 though I have come here a little late, please stay and talk to
me; it does not hurt me, and I am burning up!

25 If you just recently came into this blind world from the good
Italian earth from which my guilt comes,

let me know if Romagna is at peace or war; I was from the   28
mountain region there between Urbino and that ridge where the
Tiber flows forth."

Still I was bending over and listening to him when my leader   31
poked me and said, "You talk to him, for he is an Italian."

I, my response already formulated, said without delay, "Soul,   34
hidden deep within,

Romagna is not now and has never been without war in the   37
minds of its evil leaders; but when I left, there was no open war.

Ravenna is the same as it has been for several years: The eagle   40
from Polenta covers it and Cervia with its wings.

The city that endured a long trial, and made the French into   43
a bloody mess, now is in its green claws.

The mastiffs of Verrucchio, both the young and old, who   46
poorly guarded Montagna, used their teeth like they have always.

Lamone and Santerno are being led by the young lion from   49
the white nest, who changes sides from summer to winter.

The city which is bound on one side by the Savio, just as it is   52
between the plains and the mountains, so it is between tyranny
and freedom.

Now I beg you, say who you are. Be kinder now than others   55
have been to you, so that your name may be better in the world."

The flame roared a bit, as fires do, moving its tongue back   58
and forth, and then said,

"If I thought that I were speaking to one who could ever go   61
back to the world, this flame would stay without shaking;

64   but since no one has ever gone out from this place alive, or so I have been told, I will answer you without fear of gaining a bad name.

67   I was a soldier, then later, a Franciscan, thinking that by it I would be made right; surely this would have happened

70   if not for the high priest. May Hell have him! He brought me back to my original sins; I want you to hear from me how and why this happened.

73   While still I had the flesh and bone my mother gave me, I did not do the work of a lion, but of a fox.

76   I knew all the tricks, and so I used them so well I was famous throughout the earth.

79   When I reached that point in life when a man should lower the sails and coil the ropes,

82   those tricks that had made me happy now upset me, and I became repentant; (how miserable I am!) and it should have worked.

85   However, the prince of the new Pharisees, who was warring near the Lateran, but not against the Saracens or Jews,

88   for his enemies were all Christians, and none of them were conquerors of Acre or a trader in the Sultan's lands,

91   had no respect for his office or his holy orders, nor my cord, which tended to make its wearers thinner.

94   But like how Constantine asked Sylvester of Soracte to cure his leprosy, so he asked me how

97   to cure his fever of pride; I was silent, for he spoke like a drunken man.

So he said again, 'Do not fear, I will forgive you, if you show   100
me how to burn Palestrina to the ground.

I can lock and unlock Heaven, as you are aware; this is why   103
there are two keys, which my predecessor did not honor.'

So his strong argument moved me, for my silence seemed the   106
worst response, and I said, 'Father, since you forgive

the sin I must now commit, a long promise and short keeping   109
will bring your throne victory.'

Francis came later for me, when I died. But, one of the black   112
angels said to him, 'Do not take him. Do no wrong to me.

He must come down with my slaves, because he gave bad   115
counsel; from then to now I have been watching him;

no man can be forgiven if he does not repent, neither can   118
one both repent and do evil, because that contradiction is not
allowed.'

How wretched I am! How I shook when he grabbed me,   121
saying, 'Perhaps, you did not think I understood that logic!'

He took me to Minos; he twisted his tail around his back   124
eight times, and after he bit it in rage,

he said, 'This one deserves stealing fire!' So now I am lost   127
here where you see me, and I am clothed in this way, in torment."

When he finished speaking, the flame went off, twisting and   130
beating about.

We went farther, my leader and I, along the ridge to the next   133
bridge, which goes over the ditch where the payment is collected

from those who profited by creating division.   136

Canto XXVII Notes

Ulysses and Diomedes depart, and Virgil and Dante are approached by another flame. The spirit questions Dante about Romagna, his hometown; Dante tells him that the region is not in open warfare at the time, and then questions as to the soul's identity. The spirit reveals himself as Guido da Montefeltro, a soldier turned friar. Thinking that Dante is a condemned soul, he tells him the story of his fall to sin.

7-15. Sicilian bull: According to tradition, the metal-worker Perillos designed a bull of bronze as a torture and execution device that was used by Phalaris, a ruler in Sicily. A person could be locked inside the bull, and a fire was lit underneath, causing the person to be roasted alive. An intricate system of tubes caused the cries of the tortured to come out sounding like a bull. Phalaris then tested the bull by placing Perillos inside; either he was killed from the fire or else Phalaris removed him, near death, and threw him off a hill.

28-30. Romagna: Romagna was a coastal region in northern Italy: Urbino is a town in the eastern part of Romagna, and the Tiber is the river that originated in Romagna and flowed south: the location referred to is the Coronaro mountain range.

37-54. (various): In this extensive section, Dante tells the condition of eight Italian cities that were being ruled by tyrants; only Italians with an extensive understanding of the politics of the time would understand Dante's confusing speech.

67-123. soldier...Franciscan: We find that the spirit is Guido da Montefeltro, an accomplished soldier and strategist; he was actually called 'the fox' on account of his cunningness. Late in life, though, he regretted his actions and became a monk to pay for his sins. When Boniface VIII (whom Guido calls both 'the high priest' and 'the prince of the new Pharisees') became pope following Celestine V's resignation, the powerful Colonna family opposed Boniface's right to the papacy, and secured themselves in the fortress at Palestrina, near the Lateran, a collection of buildings owned by the Church. Boniface asked for Guido's advice on how to destroy the fortress, promising Guido that he would forgive him of his sin of providing this advice. Guido said that Boniface should grant amnesty to the Colonnas, and then burn the fortress down when they left. Believing the pope's promise, Guido never repented of his sin. Upon death, Saint Francis came to take him to heaven, but a demon came and took him instead.

85-90. Saracens or Jews...Acre...Sultan: Boniface waged war against the Colonnas, members of the Catholic church, rather than opponents to the faith, such as the Saracens who fought the Crusaders at Acre, or the Jews, who did business in the land of the Sultan.

94. Constantine...Sylvester of Soracte: Constantine, who was briefly mention in Canto 19, persecuted Christians, forcing Pope Sylvester I to hide in a cave in Soracte, a mountain ridge near Rome. However, when Constantine acquired leprosy, he had Sylvester brought to him; when Sylvester cured him, Constantine became Christian and adopted Christianity as the religion of the Roman Empire.

C A N T O   X X V I I I

1   Who could ever, even with a limitless number of words, fully explain all the blood and wounds I saw, even if he could try many times?

4   Any tongue that tried would certainly fail, for human language and understanding are too weak to understand so much.

7   If someone gathered together all the people who, crying, poured out their blood

10   because of the Trojans at Apulia, and those in the long war that claimed many mounds of rings, as Livy, who makes no mistake, wrote about,

13   and all those who were wounded while resisting Robert Guiscard, and those whose bones are still being gathered

16   at Ceperano, where every Apulian lied, and at Tagliacozzo, where the old Elard defeated without weapons;

19   if they were all collected, and one showed his ripped limb, and another his limb cut off, that still would not even begin to compare to the hideousness of the ninth ditch.

22   A barrel having lost a ring or bottom is not even as broken as one man I saw there, who was torn open from his chin to his farting-hole.

His intestines were dangling between his legs; his pluck   25
could be seen, as well as the awful bag that makes shit out of
what we eat.

While I was still amazed by looking at him, he, looking back   28
at me, opened up his chest with his hands, and said, "Now see
how I split myself!

See how Mohammed is torn open! Ali goes crying in front of   31
me, his face is split from his chin to his hair.

All the others you see here created scandals and division in   34
life, and so they are divided in this way.

Back there is a demon that cuts us so horribly, who puts his   37
sword to us

after every circle we make on this road of pain, for before we   40
meet him each time our wounds close up again.

But, who are you mocking us from on the bridge, perhaps so   43
you may delay the punishment for your own crimes?"

"Death has not yet taken him, and guilt" my master answered,   46
"has not yet delivered him to torment; but, so he may experience
everything,

I, who have died, must guide him through all of Hell, from   49
circle to circle; everything I tell you is true."

Over a hundred of them, upon hearing him, stopped to look   52
up at us, forgetting their suffering for a short while.

"Now, you who will see the sun again soon, tell Brother   55
Dolcino, if he does not want to come down here with me,

to pack enough food that the snow does not give the Novarese   58
a victory, which would otherwise be difficult for them to get."

61 Mohammed spoke these words to me with his foot lifted, as if to walk off; once he had spoken, he put it down and left.

64 Another spirit, who had a hole in his throat, his nose sliced up to his eyebrows, and only one ear,

67 stopped to look with amazement with the others, and was the first of them to open his windpipe, which was covered in red blood,

70 said, "You who are not punished by guilt, whom I saw in Italy, if I am not deceived,

73 do not forget Pier of Medicina, if you ever go back to the plains sloping from Vercelli to Marcabò.

76 Tell the two best men in Fano, Guido and Angiolello, that, if my prediction is correct,

79 they will be tossed from their ship in a loaded sack and drowned near Cattolica, thanks to a wicked tyrant betraying them.

82 Neptune has never seen such a horrible sin done between Cyprus and Maiolica, by pirates or Argolians.

85 The traitor who sees with one eye, who controls the city my companion wished he still was in,

88 will have them come to some safety; he will make it that they need no oaths or prayers against the Focara wind."

91 I said to him, "Tell me, if you want me to tell them this news, who the one is with the bad sight?"

94 So he put his hand on the mouth of one of his companions and opened his mouth for him, crying out, "This is he, who cannot speak.

He was an exile, and destroyed Caesar's doubts, proving that   97
one who is prepared always is hurt by a delay."

How saddened Curio appeared, with his tongue cut out, who   100
was so strong in speaking!

One who had both his hands cut off, lifted the stumps so that   103
the blood went all over his face,

cried out, "You will also remember Mosca, who said, 'What   106
is done is done,' the root of all evil for Tuscans."

I added to his thought, "And your clan." So he, with more   109
griefs now added, went on a like a man mad with sadness.

I stayed to look at the remainder of them, and I saw something   112
I fear to tell again, even if I had more proof of it;

but I am strengthened by conscience, that good friend that   115
frees men, knowing it is pure.

I certainly saw, and I almost still see, a body without a head   118
walking just like the others of the sad group;

he was holding up his severed head by the hair, swinging   121
back and forth like a lantern; the head was looking at us, saying,
"O me!"

He made himself a lamp for himself; they were two in one   124
and one in two; how that can be true, he who says so knows.

When he was right under the bridge, he raised up his arm,   127
head and all, so we could better hear his words,

which were: "See my awful punishment now, you who   130
go about watching the dead while still breathing; see if any
punishment is as great as this!

133   And so you can take back news of me, I am Bertran de Born, who gave bad advice to the young king.

136   I made father and son fight against each other: What Achitophel did to Absalom and David with his evil advice is no worse than what I did.

139   Because I split two persons so connected, I hold my brain split from its source, the trunk.

142   So you can see in me the counter-punishment."

Canto XXVIII Notes

Dante and Virgil climb the bridge over the ninth ditch, where they find the schismatics, the sowers of discord. Among them he finds the Islamic prophet Mohammed and his cousin Ali, as well as Pier da Medicina, Gaius Scribonius Curio, Mosca de' Lamberti, and Bertran de Born.

1-142. THE SCHISMATICS: The sinners in the ninth bolgia are the schismatics, or sowers of discord, whose actions caused divisions within religion, country, and family. Fittingly, they walk around the circle and pass by a demon who cuts them; as they walk, their wounds heal until they are cut again.

10. Trojans at Apulia: Several bloody wars were fought between the Trojans and the peoples in Apulia, which generally refers to the southern part of Italy.

10-12. long war...rings...Livy: Livy was a famous Roman historian; the 'long war' referred to is the Second Punic War, in which Hannibal collected many golden rings from the corpses of the dead Romans.

14. Robert Guiscard: Guiscard fought for twenty years to gain control of Apulia.

16. Ceperano...Apulian: This refers to a battle at Ceperano, where Manfred, the king of Sicily, was defeated when the Apulians deserted him.

17-18. Tagliacozzo...Elard: The Ghibellines were defeated in a battle at Tagliacozzo, where the general Elard de Valéry won through his clever tactics (rather than weapons).

31. Mohammed...Ali: Dante was of the opinion that Mohammed was a Christian who formed a competing religion, Islam, causing a large number of Christians to fall from the faith. Ali was his son-in-law and cousin whose eventual replacement of Mohammed resulted in Islam's division into the Sunni and Shia branches.

55-60. Brother Dolcino...Novarese: Mohammed here prophesies about Brother Dolcino, who was the leader of the so-called 'Apostolic Brethren' (mostly from Novara in northern Italy) who condemned the current papacy and hoped to renew the church. Pope Clement V ordered them to be captured; this happened when they ran out of food and began to starve after two years.

73. Pier of Medicina: It is not known who he is, though it is thought that he is likely Piero di Aimo da Medicina; he is the one speaking.

74-75. plains...Vercelli...Marcabò: That is, the valley of the Po river.

76-81. Fano...Guido...Angiolello...Cattolica: Pier prophesies the death of Guido del Cassero and Angiolello di Carignano, two leaders of Fano, a town in eastern Italy. They were killed when the tyrant Malatestino Malatesta tricked them into meeting at Cattolica, a town near Fano, where they were drowned in sacks.

82-84. Neptune...Cyprus...Majorca: That is to say, no sin so great was ever done in the Mediterranean Sea.

85-90. traitor...Focara wind: This is still referring to the previous prophecy: Malatesta, who had only one eye, would control the city of Rimini, which Malatesta's companion (who we will find is Curio) wishes he'd never seen. The waters near

Cattolica were dangerous, and prayers were often made in navigating them. When Cassero and Carignano would be dead, they would have no need to pray.

97-102. Caesar's doubts...Curio: Curio was the one who advised Caesar to cross the Rubicon, thus starting the civil wars in Rome.

106-109. Mosca...Tuscans...clan: When an influential member of the Buondelmonti family broke off his engagement to a girl from the Amidei family, Mosca suggested that Amidei seek revenge; this eventually led to the division between the Guelfs and Ghibellines.

133-136. Bertran de Born...young king: One account of Bertran de Born, a lord, tells that he attempted to create war between King Henry II and his second son.

138-139. Achitophel...Absalom...David: According to II Samuel, Achitophel was a counselor to King David who encouraged David's son Absalom to rebel against his father, which ultimately led to Absalom's death.

142. counter-punishment: The counter-punishment is the method of punishment in the *Inferno:* That each sinner be punished in the same way in which he sinned.

Canto XXIX

1   The great number of people, and their unusual wounds, had so captured my eyes that I wished to stay and weep.

4   But Virgil said to me, "Why are you still staring? Why do you still watch those dismembered spirits down there?

7   You didn't act like this at the other ditches; if you hope to count them all, this ditch is twenty-two miles around.

10   Now the moon is beneath us; we have little of the time we have been given, and there is much yet for you to see."

13   "If you'd considered," I answered, "why I was staring, then perhaps you would have allowed me to stay longer."

16   While I was speaking, my leader went on, and I added, "In that ditch

19   where I was looking, I think a relative of mine is weeping for the guilt that is punished down there."

22   Then my master said, "Do not let your mind think of him again. Think on other things, and let him stay there;

25   I saw him under the bridge; he was pointing at you threateningly, and I heard someone call him Geri de Bello.

But then your attention went to him who once ruled   28
Hautefort, and you did not look at him, so he went on."

"My leader, his death, which is unavenged," I said, "by   31
anyone who shares shame for it,

has made him so angry; so, he went off without speaking to   34
me, and that makes me feel more compassion for him."

So we talked while walking, until we reached the point   37
where we would have first been able to see into the next ditch,
had there been more light.

So when we were above the last ditch of Malebolge, where   40
we would have seen its spirits,

strange cries came to me, like arrows with heads made of   43
pity, so I covered my ears.

Imagine all the suffering of the sick in the hospitals of   46
Valdichiana between July and September, and also from
Maremma and Sardinia,

put in one ditch together; that is what it was, and a smell like   49
rotting flesh rose from it.

We went down to the last ridge from the long bridge, still   52
moving to the left; and then I could see down

to the bottom, where Justice, the Lord's minister, punishes   55
the falsifiers.

I do not think it was even a greater sadness to see all the sick   58
people in Aegina, when there was so much malice

that all animals, even the tiniest worm, died (and the ancient   61
peoples, so the poets say,

64 came from ants), than to see all the spirits piled in heaps in the dark valley.

67 One was laying over another, one over another's shoulders, one crawling down the road.

70 We went on, not talking, watching and hearing those sick sinners, who could not stand up.

73 I saw two sinners sitting up against each, like how two pans can be propped up against each other to cool; they were covered in scabs from head to toe.

76 I have never seen a currycomb so quickly used by a boy waiting for his master, or one who was very tired,

79 as each of the sinners scratched at himself with his fingernails, because of the horrible itch; but this no longer was a comfort.

82 Their nails cut off the scabs like knives scaling a fish with large scales.

85 "You who skin yourself with your fingers," my master said to one of them, "and sometimes use them like claws,

88 tell us if there are any Italians in here, so you may go about with your nails for eternity."

91 "Both of us are Italians, so wasted here," one said, weeping, "but who are you to be asking about us?"

94 My leader said to him, "I am going from each ridge to the next with a living man; I intend to show him all of Hell."

97 Then their support of each other went away, and each turned to me, trembling, along with all the others who heard, as if because of an echo.

My good master came near to me and said, "Tell them what   100
you have to say." And I said, because he wished it,

"In order that your legacy may not be lost from human   103
minds, so that it may live on,

tell me your name and your people; do not let your disgusting   106
punishment scare you from telling me."

One of them said, "I was from Arezzo. Alberto of Siena was   109
the one that killed me by fire; but, the reason for my death is not
the sin that sent me here.

It is true that I said to him, joking, 'I could fly in the air,' and   112
he, who was very eager but had no common sense,

asked me to show him. Only because I could not make him a   115
Daedalus, he had one who loved him like a son burn me to death.

But Minos, who cannot make a mistake, sent me to this last   118
ditch of the ten, for alchemy, which I did in life."

I said to my poet, "Was there ever a people who were as   121
foolish as the Sienese? Even the French were not; by far!"

The other leper, hearing me, said, "Except Stricca, who spent   124
moderately,

and Nicholas, who was the first to discover the trade of   127
cloves, in the place where they grow,

and except that crew which Caccia d'Asciano used his   130
vineyard and farms, and to whom Abbagliato showed off his
great wisdom.

But so you may know who is second to you against the   133
Sienese, look to me, so my face can answer you:

136   you will see that I am Capocchio, who falsified with metals in
alchemy; you surely remember, if I know who you are,

139   how well I imitated nature."

CANTO XXIX NOTES

As Virgil urges Dante to continue, Dante wishes to stay back shortly, having seen a relative of his. They then progress to the bridge over the final bolgia, where the falsifiers suffer from many diseases and a foul stench rises. Virgil asks whether there are any Italians, and Dante speaks with both Griffolino and Capocchio.

27. Geri de Bello: Geri de Bello was Dante's second cousin.

28-29. him who once ruled Hautefort: That is, Bertran de Born, with whom Dante spoke in Canto 28.

40-139. FALSIFIERS: The falsifiers (who are divided into several groups) are punished in the tenth and final bolgia. They are afflicted with a variety of gross illnesses and depravities. Canto 29 deals with the first group of falsifiers, the alchemists. Canto 30 will deal with impersonators, counterfeiters, and false witnesses.

46-48. Valdichiana...Maremma...Sardinia: These regions in Italy were especially hard-hit with cases of malaria during the warm months.

59-66. Aegina...animals...ancient peoples: According to tradition, Juno sent a plague to the land of Aegina, causing all the people and animals to die, except for the king, Aeacus. When he prayed to the gods, Juno repopulated the island by turning the ants into people.

109-117. Arezzo...Alberto of Siena: This is Griffolino, who apparently was killed after promising such things to Alberto of Siena as teaching him how to fly (as it was said Daedalus could). Alberto had the bishop (the one who loved Alberto as a son) burn Griffolino at the stake. He is punished here, however, for his sins of alchemy.

124-132. Stricca...Nicholas...Caccia...Abbagliato: This other sinner sarcastically refers to four famous Sienese wasters. Caccia and Abbagliato were two members of the so-called 'Spend-Thrift Brigade,' who gathered their fortunes and wasted them away partying in under two years.

136. Capocchio: Little is known about him, other than that he was burned at the stake for alchemy in 1293. He may have been a student with Dante.

CANTO XXX

1   In the time when Juno was angry at the Thebans, because of Semele, as she expressed many times,

4   Athamas lost his mind so that, when he saw his wife with his two sons,

7   he yelled out, "Spread a net, so I can capture the lioness and her cubs at the crossway!" And then he put out his claws,

10   snatching up Learchus, and threw him up against a rock, hitting his head; she drowned herself with her other son.

13   When Fortune had set the pride of the Trojans to the ground, aflame, so that the king was destroyed with his kingdom,

16   Hecuba, sorrowful and a captive, after seeing Polyxena dead, and had grieved over seeing Polydorus on the shore,

19   she went mad, and barked like a dog, for her sorrow had so broken her mind.

22   But neither Furies from Thebes nor Trojans ever made someone so evil, not to hurt beasts or people,

25   as two naked spirits I saw, who were biting like pigs let loose.

28   One, when he reached Capocchio, stabbed his neck with his tusk, and dragged him on his belly across the ground.

The Arentine, who was still standing there trembling, said,   31
"That goblin's name is Gianni Schicchi; he goes about abusing
others in his rage."

I said to him, "So that the other one may not bite you, let me   34
know who he is before he disappears."

He said to me, "That spirit is Myrrha, who became her   37
father's lover, going beyond appropriate love.

She sinned with him by hiding herself with the appearance   40
of another, just like the other spirit there,

who, to get the queen of the herd, dared to pretend to be   43
Buoso Donati, and made a legal will."

When the two violent spirits, which I had been watching,   46
went off, I looked at the others.

I saw one whose body had been made to look like a lute (if   49
his legs were cut off).

The dropsy that deforms the organs with the bad liquid it   52
forms, so the face does not respond to the requests of the stomach,

made him keep his mouth open, like a fevered person who   55
holds the top lip up and the lower lip down in thirst.

"You who are not punished, thought I do not know why you   58
would not be in this sad world," he said, "see

the wretched form of Master Adam; when I was alive, I got   61
everything I asked for. Now, I crave just a drop of water.

The streams that go from Casentino to Arno, cool and moist,   64

I can always see in my mind, and that thought dries me even   67
more than the disease that destroys the skin of my face.

70 The Justice that punishes me does so with the images of the place where I sinned, so I sigh even more often.

73 I see Romena, where I counterfeited the metal with the seal of the Baptist; for that, I left my body burned up there.

76 But if I may see the spirit of Guido or Alessandro, or their brother, I would not trade that sight, even for Fonte Branda.

79 One of them has already come here, if the spirits that run around here tell the truth; but what use is that to me, since my limbs are tied?

82 If even I could walk one inch in a hundred years, I would have already started the journey of

85 searching through these people, though this ditch is eleven miles around, and certainly no less than half a mile wide.

88 It is because of them that I am in such a house; they were the ones that made me counterfeit the florins that had three carats of waste in them."

91 I said to him, "Who are those two spirits steaming like wet hands in cold air, close to your right?"

94 "I found them here, and because they have never moved since I came down to this pit," he said, "I do not think they ever will.

97 One is the fake woman who blamed Joseph; the other is a fake Greek, Sinon from Troy. They give off such a stench because of their bad fever."

100 One of them, who perhaps was angered at being named so unkindly, struck Master Adams' belly with his fist.

103 It made a noise like a drum, and Master Adam hit the other's face with his arm, which was no softer,

saying, "Though my heavy limbs prevent me from walking, I   106
have one arm loose for such uses as this!"

The other replied, "When you were sentenced to the fire,   109
you weren't so quick with it; but you had that and more when
you were counterfeiting!"

The swollen one said, "You tell the truth, but you did not   112
when you were asked for the truth in Troy."

"I may have spoken falsely, but you falsified coins," Sinon   115
said, "but I am here for just one sin. You are here for more sins
than any other demon!"

"Remember the Horse, you perjurer," replied the one with   118
the swollen belly, "and may you suffer that the whole world
knows about it!"

To that the Greek said, "I hope the thirst that cracks your   121
tongue is always bitter, and that your stagnant juices make your
belly a hedge before your face!"

The coiner said, "Your mouth is gaping as it always does from   124
your disease; while I am thirsty, and yet liquid swells me up,

you have a burning fever and a bad headache; so you would   127
lick the mirror of Narcissus just as quickly as I!"

I was hoping to listen to them longer, but my master said   130
to me, "If you keep watching, the two of us will not be far from
quarreling!"

When I heard his angry words, I turned to him in a shame   133
that I still feel.

Like one dreaming of pain, and dreaming, wishes he were   136
dreaming that what is happening were not,

139   so I was like, and I was making excuses for myself the whole time, though not realizing it.

142   "A little bit of shame can wash away even a greater fault," my master said, "than yours, so do not be sorrowful.

145   Remember that I have always been with you if you ever again are in a situation where Fortune puts you with arguing people:

148   To wish to hear their fighting is a very vulgar desire."

Canto XXX Notes

Still in the tenth bolgia, Dante witnesses Gianni Schicchi and Myrrha, impersonators who run around the ditch and attack other sinners. He also sees Master Adam, a counterfeiter of money, as well as Potiphar's wife and Sinon, who were false witnesses. Sinon and Master Adam engage in a battle of accusations and physical attacks, which Dante hopes to stay and watch, but Virgil rebukes him.

1-12. Semele...Athamas...Learchus: When Juno was jealous of Semele, the daughter of the founder of Thebes, she killed Semele. In addition, Juno caused Athamas, the husband of Semele's sister Ino, to go into a rage in which he killed Learchus, one of his sons, which caused Ino to throw herself and her other child into the sea to drown.

13-21. Hecuba...Polyxena...Polydorus: Hecuba, the queen of Troy, was carried off from Troy after it fell, and saw her daughter Polyxena sacrificed by the Greeks. When she went to the sea to get water to prepare the body for burial, she found the corpse of her son Polydorus washed up on shore, causing her to go mad.

31. Arentine: Griffolino, mentioned in Canto 29.

32. Gianni Schicchi: He was a Florentine well known for his ability to impersonate others.

37. Myrrha: She disguised herself so as to sleep with her father, the king of Cyprus.

43-45. *queen...Buoso Donati:* According to this story, Schicchi pretended to be the recently dead Buoso Donati in order to forge a will that would grant the inheritance to the Schicchi family, and which granted Donati's 'queen of the herd' (his best mule) to Gianni.

61-75. *Master Adam:* Likely an Englishman, he was convinced by a family in Romena to counterfeit the florin, the currency in Florence, which bore an image of John the Baptist. He was burned at the stake for his crimes. Now punished with illness, he thirsts and is tormented by the memory of the water that runs in the Casentino range (near Florence) to the Arno, a major Italian river.

76-78. *Guido...Alessandro...Fonte Branda:* Those mentioned are members of the family that hired him to do the counterfeiting; he is told that one of them is already punished, but cannot move due to his disease. He would rather see them punished in Hell than be able to drink from the Fonte Branda (a now unknown spring).

90. *three carats of waste:* Florins were made of twenty-four carats of gold, and Adam counterfeited them by using only twenty-one carats of gold and three of some other metal.

97. *fake woman who blamed Joseph:* This is Potiphar's wife. According to Genesis, she wished to sleep with him and he refused, so she accused him of attempting to rape her.

98. *Sinon from Troy:* When the Greeks left the Trojan horse outside Troy, they also left Sinon, who pretended to be a sacrifice to the Trojans. When the Horse was taken into Troy, Sinon released the Greeks inside.

100. *one of them:* We will see it is Sinon.

128-129. *mirror of Narcissus:* According to the well-known myth, Narcissus fell in love with himself when he saw his reflection in a pool of water. Now, though Sinon and Adam have different diseases, they both suffer from extreme thirst.

C ANTO X X X I

1   The tongue that had first stung me, my cheeks blushing in shame, then gave me a medicine:

4   So I have heard was the case with the spear of Achilles and his father, which first gave harm, and then healing.

7   We turned our backs to that sad ditch, and went across the ridge that circles it, without saying anything more.

10   Here it was not night, nor day, so I could not see very far ahead; but I heard a horn, so loud

13   that it would make any thunder ashamed. The sound of it caused me to turn to look at one place.

16   After the sad defeat in which Charlemagne lost his holy army, and Roland sounded his horn, even that was not so awful a sound.

19   I was not looking in that direction for long before I seemed to see many tall towers, so I said, "Master, tell me, what is this city?"

22   And he said, "Because you are looking too far into the shadows, your sight is blurry.

25   When it becomes clearer, you will understand how sight can be tricked by great distance; so go on a little farther."

So he took my hand kindly and said, "Before we go closer, so   28
you may not be so frightened,

know that they are actually giants. They are standing in the   31
pit, all the way around, so that they are only seen from their
bellies up."

Just like how one can make out little by little what the haze   34
has hidden when it finally goes away,

so, traveling through the thick, dark air, getting closer to the   37
edge, my mistaken image left and my fear grew;

for, just as Montereggione's walls have many towers lining   40
them, so the terrible giants towered over the plain that circles
the pit,

half their bodies shown, those giants Jove still threatens with   43
thunder.

Already I could make out one of them, his face and his   46
shoulders, and his chest and most of his belly, and both his arms.

Nature was surely good to not create such creatures for Mars   49
to have!

And while she still makes elephants and whales, whoever   52
looks on them will consider her more just and careful for it;

for when keenness and evil are joined, men cannot defend   55
themselves against that.

His face looked as long and wide as Peter's pine cone in   58
Rome, and his bones were in that same unusual proportion;

so that the pit, which was like an apron on his waist, left so   61
much visible that three Frisians would have no need to boast

64   of being able to reach his hair, for I saw it was thirty large spans down from where one would put a belt.

67   "Raphèl maì amècche zabì almì," were the words which he shouted, for there was no gentle song for him.

70   My leader yelled to him, "You stupid spirit, be happy with your horn; use that when anger or passion overcomes you!

73   The strap that holds it is around your neck, you dumb soul; there it is laying across your chest."

76   Then he said to me, "He accuses himself; he is Nimrod; it was because of his evil thought that the world no longer speaks the same language.

79   Let's leave him, so not to waste speech, for all human languages are to him like his to humans: babbling."

82   So we took a longer path, moving to the left; we saw the next giant, much fiercer and bigger, about an arrow's shot away.

85   Who was the master that could contain him, I cannot say, but one arm was tied in front, and the other in back,

88   by a chain that went down from his neck around his body five times.

91   "This prideful one tried to show his power against Jove," my leader explained, "and so he is rewarded.

94   He is Ephialtes, and he did many great things when giants still scared the gods; the arm he used to strike now can never move."

97   I said to him, "If it is at all possible, I would like to be able to see Briareus, the massive one."

He replied, "Very close you can see Antaeus, who is able to   100
speak and is not bound; he will lift us and put us down at the
bottom of all this evil.

The one you wish to see is very much farther away; he is   103
bound in the same way and looks very much the same, though
his face seems angrier."

A horrid earthquake could never shake a tower quite as   106
violently as Ephialtes shook himself without warning.

More than ever before I feared death, and that alone would   109
have been enough to kill me, if not for my being able to see his
chains.

We went farther and arrived at Antaeus, who rose a good   112
five ells above the ledge, without his head.

"You, who, in the good valley that made Scipio an heir to   115
glory after Hannibal and his army ran away,

captured a thousand lions, and, had you fought in your   118
brother's great war,

the sons of earth may have found victory, or so some say: Set   121
us down in the place where the cold freezes Cocytus, and do so
kindly.

Do not force us to go to Tityos or Typhon; this man can give   124
you what you want; so bend down and do not be angered.

He can pay you with fame in the world, for he is still alive   127
and anticipates living for many more years, if grace does not call
him away before his days are done."

So my master said, and he who once held Hercules, grabbed   130
on to my leader.

133   Virgil, when he was gripped, said to me, "Come over here, so I can hold you." So he made the both of us into one bundle.

136   Just as the Garisenda appears to fall over when viewed from the leaning side when a cloud passes over it,

139   so Antaeus seemed to do when I watched, waiting for him to bend, and then I wished I could have taken some other road!

142   But he set us down lightly at the bottom that eats up Lucifer and Judas; he did not stay bent over,

145   but rose up like the mast of a ship.

Canto XXXI Notes

Dante and Virgil now progress out of the eighth circle and toward a central pit, the bottom of which is the frozen lake Cocytus and the ninth and final circle of Hell. Several giants stand at the bottom of the pit, and their waists rise above the edge of the pit. Virgil points out Nimrod, Ephialtes, Briareus, Tityos, Typhon, and Antaeus. Antaeus lowers Dante and Virgil down the floor of the pit.

4-6. spear of Achilles: Legend told that Achilles' spear could heal a wound it caused. It was incorrectly thought by Dante and others at the time that the spear had belonged to Achilles' father.

16-18. Charlemagne...Roland: Roland was in charge of Charlemagne's rear guard; when they were ambushed, Roland blew his horn for help, but it was too late, and they were all killed.

21. this city: Dante mistakes the giants for watchtowers.

40. Montereggione: A small fortress that still stands today. Dante compares the appearance of the giants to the walls of the fortress.

43. Jove: That is, Jupiter, who drove away the giants when they attacked Mount Olympus.

50. Mars: The god of war.

58. pine cone: A large bronze pine cone that had been located in Rome. It is around a dozen feet tall.

58-66. Frisians...thirty large spans: Dante makes an attempt to describe the size of the giants, relating them both to the height of Frisians (considered a strong and large race) and a span (the distance between the end of the thumb and pinky in a spread hand). All in all, the giants are probably somewhere around 70 feet tall.

67. "Raphèl maì amècche zabì almì": Many commentators have attempted to interpret these words, but there is no agreement upon their meaning. I prefer to think that, along with Plutus' speech, they are intended to be meaningless.

76-78. Nimrod...his evil thought: Genesis tells the account of the building of the tower of Babel, where man attempted to build a tower to reach to heaven. In response, God caused them to speak many different languages, causing them to scatter and populate the world. Tradition held that Nimrod was the one that started the idea for the tower.

91-96. Jove...Ephialtes: Ephialtes was the son of Neptune and was sent by him to pile two mountains on top of each other to reach Olympus and throw out Jove and the gods.

99. Briareus: Traditionally a hundred-handed giant, though this is evidently not the case in the *Inferno*.

100. Antaeus: A giant killed by Hercules.

114. five ells: About eight feet.

115-117. good valley...Scipio: Zama, a region in Africa, where Scipio defeated Hannibal's forces and Rome gained control of the Mediterranean.

120-121. your brother's great war: That is to say, had Antaeus fought with the giants against the gods, the giants would have likely won.

123. Cocytus: The frozen river that forms the ninth circle of Hell.

124. Tityos or Typhon: Both were giants that fought against the gods.

130. once held Hercules: That is, when Antaeus and Hercules fought each other.

136. Garisenda: A tower in Bologna that leans considerably. Dante compares the sight of Antaeus lowering them to how towers appear to tip over when one watches the moving clouds above them.

143. Lucifer and Judas: That is, Satan and Judas Iscariot, who reside at the very center of Hell. We will see them in Canto 34.

Canto XXXII

1   If I had harsh rhymes, which would be fitting for this horrid hole to which all weight is focused,

4   I would make a greater effort to explain my concept; but because I do not, I speak of it with fear,

7   for to describe the bottom of the universe is no task to be taken easily, and it is not one for a tongue that says, "mommy" or "daddy."

10   But let those ladies who helped Amphion hold up Thebes help me in my writing so that the words I use may not be far off from what I describe.

13   You who are in this indescribable place, it would be better for you, even more than others, to have been sheep or goats!

16   When finally we were down in the dark pit, below the feet of the giants, and while still I was looking at the tall cliff,

19   one of them said to me, "Watch your steps! Walk carefully, so you do not kick any of the heads of your tired, forsaken brothers."

22   I then turned, and saw all around me a lake that the cold had given a glassy appearance, rather than watery.

25   The Austrian Danube, and the Don beneath the cold sky, never made so thick a veil as was in this place;

I think, had Mount Tamberlic or the mountain in Pietrapana   28
fallen on it, it would not even have made a creak at the edges!

As a frog sits with its nose out of the water, during the season   31
in which the peasant woman wishes she could gather,

so the sad, pale shades were encased in the ice up to the part   34
of the body that shows shame, making the song of a stork with
their teeth.

Each of them held their faces down; their mouths were   37
showing the great cold; their eyes showing their great shame.

After I had look around, I then looked down, and saw two   40
who were so pressed against each other that their hair was tangled
together.

"Tell me, you who press your chests together," I said, "who   43
are you?" They bent their heads back, and when they looked at
me,

their eyes, which until then had only been wet, gave off tears   46
that dripped all over, and the cold froze their eyes, locking them
shut.

A clamp has never held two boards so tight; like two goats,   49
they started butting heads, for they had such anger.

Another, whose ears were both gone due to frostbite, with   52
his face turned down, said, "Why do you still look at us?

If you are wondering who these two are, they and their   55
father, Albert, owned the valley from which the Bisenzio flows.

They were born from the same body; if you search through   58
all Caina, you will not find a single spirit more worthy of being
encased in this ice,

61   not even he whose chest and soul were pierced in a single blow by Arthur; not Focaccia, and not this one, whose head blocks my vision,

64   whose name was Sassol Mascheroni. If you are a Tuscan, then you will know him.

67   And so I will not have to speak any more, know that my name was Camiscion de' Pazzi; I am waiting for Carlino to come here to excuse me."

70   Then I saw a thousand faces that the cold had make dog-like, and for it now I always shudder at the cold.

73   While we went walking toward the point to which all weight is centered, and while I was shaking from the everlasting cold,

76   I do not know whether it was by a wish, or destiny, or Fortune, but, while I was walking around the heads, I kicked one hard in the face.

79   Crying, it yelled at me, "Why do you attack me? If you have not come to increase the revenge of Montaperti, why are you bothering me?"

82   I said, "Master, wait for me a while, so I can free myself from doubt; then you can hurry me along as you wish."

85   My leader stopped, and I said to that sinner, who still was shouting curses, "Who are you, who goes about scolding others?"

88   "Who are you, who walks through Antenora," he said, "kicking others in the face, even more harshly than you would be entitled if you were alive?"

91   "I am alive, and that fact could be useful to you," I replied, "if you want fame, for I could mention you in my notes."

He said to me, "I want the opposite of that! Get away, and stop   94
bothering me; you are not very good at flattery in this swamp!"

Then I grabbed him by the hair and said, "If you don't tell me   97
your name, I won't leave a single hair on your head!"

He said to me, "Even though you scalp me, I will never tell   100
you who I am, even if you kick me a thousand times!"

Already I grabbed his hair and had torn out more than one   103
chunk, and he was screaming while keeping his face down,

when another spirit yelled out, "What's wrong, Bocca? Isn't   106
it enough for you to make chattering with your teeth; but now
you have to scream as well? What demon is messing with you?"

"Now," I said, "I want you to say no more, you evil traitor, for   109
I will carry back the true news of you, to shame you."

"Get lost," he said, "and say whatever you want; but don't   112
keep quiet about he whose tongue was loose just shortly ago, if
you ever get back.

He weeps over the French coins. 'I saw,' you can tell others,   115
'the one from Duera, down in the place where sinners stay cool.'

If anyone asks, 'Who else was there?', beside you there is   118
Beccheria, whose throat was sawed through by Florence.

I think Gianni de' Soldanier is over there with Ganelon and   121
Tebaldello, who snuck into Faenza in the night."

Already we had left him, when I saw two spirits frozen in   124
the same hole, so that the one's head was like a hat to the other's.

Just as the starving eat bread, so the one dug his teeth into   127
the other in the neck:

130 It was like how Tydeus gnawed at Menalippus' head in anger,
how this one did the same with the others' skull and other parts.

133 "You who show in such a beastly way your hatred toward the
one you are eating, explain to me why," I said, "by this agreement:

136 If you complain of him justly, when I know who you are and
where you are from, I will repay you in the world above,

139 if my words do not die out."

Canto XXXII Notes

Dante and Virgil now arrive at the ninth circle, which is divided into four rounds, where traitors are punished by being encased in the frozen river Cocytus. Dante sees two stuck in the ice nearly touching. When they look up at him their tears freeze and they begin butting heads. Dante moves on, only to kick a sinner in the face. Dante attacks him for awhile and then continues toward the center of Hell.

10-12. those ladies...Amphion: The Muses, who caused the poetry written by Amphion to make rocks assemble themselves into walls around Thebes.

25. Austrian Danube...Don: Two rivers that flowed into the Black Sea and froze over during the winter.

28-29. Tamberlic...Pietrapana: Two large mountains in Tuscany.

31-72. THE TRAITORS AGAINST FAMILY: The first division of the ninth circle is called Caina, after the biblical Cain who killed his brother Abel, where traitors against family are punished; their bodies except for their necks and heads are encased in the ice.

56-57. Albert...Bisenzio: The Bisenzio is a river that flows into the Arno. The region referred to was owned by Alberto of Mangona. The two sinners are his sons Napoleone and Alessandro, who killed each other over their inheritance.

61-62. not even he...Arthur: That is, Mordred, King Arthur's son. Arthur killed him after Mordred tried to lead a rebellion against Arthur.

62. Focaccia: He is Vanni de' Cancellieri, who reportedly killed several of his family.

64. Sassol Mascheroni: A Florentine who killed his uncle's son, ensuring he would get the inheritance.

68-69. Camiscion de' Pazzi...Carlino: An Italian who killed a relative to gain his castles. His relative Carlino will 'excuse' him because he is so much worse.

73-139. THE TRAITORS AGAINST COUNTRY: The second group of traitors is punished in Antenora, named after Antenor, a Trojan that aided the Greeks in the Trojan War. The sinners here are also encased in ice, but they are unable to move their necks.

80. revenge of Montaperti: The sinner is Bocca degli Abati, who fought for the Ghibellines at the Battle of Montaperti, then pretended to side with the Guelfs after the Ghibellines were driven out of Florence.

115-117. French coins...Duera: This sinner is Buoso da Duera. He was a Ghibelline who accepted a bribe from French forces and allowed them to reach Parma.

119. Beccheria: Tesauro di Beccheria, who was accused of aiding the Ghibellines after they were expelled from Florence; he was beheaded for his actions.

121. Gianni de' Soldanier: A Ghibelline who betrayed his party.

122. Ganelon: He betrayed Charlemagne at the battle referenced in Canto 31.

122-123. Tebaldello...Faenza: A Ghibelline who allowed

Guelfs to enter Faenza and massacre their enemies within, thus settling a personal grudge against them.

130. Tydeus...Menalippus: Menalippus delivered a deadly blow to Tydeus, who then killed him. Dying himself, Tydeus requested Menalippus' head and began to chew on it.

C A N T O   X X X I I I

1   That sinner then lifted his head up from his inhuman meal, wiping his mouth on the hair of the head he had destroyed.

4   Then he said, "You want me to bring back my horrid grief that still weighs on me when I think of it, even before I say it.

7   But, if what I say would bring about the infamy of the traitor I bite at, then you will see me talking and crying.

10   I do not know who you are or how you have come to this place, but I very much believe you are a Florentine from how you speak.

13   You should know that I was Count Ugolino, and that this man is the Archbishop Ruggieri: I will explain why I am a neighbor to him here.

16   The fact that, by his evil, and by trusting him, I was killed, I need not say;

19   but the thing that you could not have heard was how cruel my death was; I will tell you, and you will determine whether he brought it upon me.

22   A small window in the mew that is called Hunger because of me, where all other windows must be shut,

had already showed me several moons when I dreamed the   25
bad dream that showed the future to me:

This man was my master and my lord, hunting the wolf and   28
his cubs on the mountain that blocks the Pisans from Lucca.

With swift bitches he put Gualandi with Sismondi and   31
Lanfranchi before him.

After a short while, the father and the sons tired, and it   34
appeared to me that the sharp fangs tore them apart.

When I awoke before the rising of the sun, I heard my sons,   37
who were there with me, crying because of nightmares, and
asking for bread.

Surely you are a heartless man if already you are not crying,   40
knowing what my heart said to me; if you are not weeping, then
what can make you weep?

They were awake, and it was nearly the time when our food   43
was brought to us, and each of us was afraid because of his dream;

when I heard that they were nailing up the door at the base   46
of the tower, I looked at my sons' faces, but said nothing.

I did not cry, for my heart had so turned to stone; so they did   49
not cry, and Anselmuccio said, 'You have a strange look on your
face, father! Why?'

So I shed no tears, and I did not answer them all day and   52
night, until the sun came up the next day.

When a single ray of light entered our sad prison, and I saw   55
four faces showing my own appearance,

I bit both my hands in rage; they, thinking that I was doing   58
it out of hunger, stood up

61   and said, 'Father, it will be better for us if you eat us: You gave us our awful flesh, so now take it from us.'

64   I was quiet then, to not make them sadder; that day, and the next we said nothing; why had the hard earth not taken us?

67   On the fourth day, Gaddo threw himself down at my feet, and said, 'Father, why don't you help me?'

70   He died right there; as just as certainly as you can see me, I watched the other three fall dead one by one between the fifth and six days. I,

73   blind, had to feel around their bodies, and for two days I called out to them, even after they were dead. Then the fasting was more powerful than the grief."

76   After he said that, he took, with eyes diverted, the other's head in his teeth, which were strong like a dog's.

79   Pisa, you who are a shame to the people where 'sì' is said, because your neighbors are slow to punish you,

82   let Capraia and Gorgona move to make a block at the mouth of Arno, so that it may flood and drown every person in you!

85   For, if Count Ugolino was said to have betrayed you, you ought not to have killed his sons.

88   Their age, you new Thebes, made his sons Uguiccione and Brigata innocent, as well as the two I have already named.

91   We went farther to the place where the cold covers another group of people, whose heads are not bent down, but held back.

94   Their tears prevent them from crying there, and the sorrow which cannot be vented because of that block turns back inward and increases their pain,

for the first tears make like a knot, and fill up those cups 97
under the eyebrows.

And even though every sensation of feeling in my face had 100
left, like if by a callus,

I already felt some wind; so I said, "My master, who creates 103
this wind, if all water vapor has been driven out?"

And he explained, "Soon you will be in a place where you see 106
the answer, when you see who is giving off this breath."

One of the grievers of the ice cried out, "O you souls so evil 109
as to be sentenced to this last place,

lift the hard veils from my eyes, so I can vent the pain that 112
gathers in my heart for a while, until the tears harden again."

So I said to him, "If you want me to help you, tell me your 115
name, and I promise that if I do not help you, I ought to be sent
down into the ice."

He answered, "I am Brother Alberigo, I am the one of the 118
fruits from the evil orchard; here I am paid a date for every fig."

"Oh," I said to him, "so you are already dead?" He said to me, 121
"I do not know what is happening to my body up there.

That sometimes happens in Ptolomea, that a soul falls here 124
before Atropos sends it.

And so you may be more willing to remove the glassy tears 127
from my eyes, know that as soon as the souls betrays,

just like I did, a demon takes the body over, who then 130
controls it until its time arrives;

the soul comes into this place. Perhaps the body of this spirit 133
behind me is still up on earth;

136   you surely know who he is, if you just came down here recently; he is Ser Branca Doria, and it has been years since he became encased like that."

139   "I think," I told him, "that you are lying to me, for Branca Doria is still alive, and he eats, drinks, and wears clothes."

142   "In the ditch," he said, "of the Malebranche, where the sticky pitch boils, Michel Zanche had not yet come,

145   when this one left earth with a devil in his place, in his body and the body of a relative who helped commit the betrayal.

148   So now take your hand and open my eyes." I did not open his eyes, and it was truly good to treat him so poorly.

151   You men of Genoa, unaware of all decent actions, and full of every vice, why have you not yet been killed off?

154   For I found with the worst of Romagna one of yours, who, for his actions already bathes in Cocytus,

157   and still is alive in his body up there.

CANTO XXXIII NOTES

Still observing the two spirits, Dante finds that they are Count Ugolino and Archbishop Ruggieri, fellow traitors. Ugolino recounts the story of his death at the hand of Ruggieri. Dante and Virgil depart and reach the third round of the ninth circle, where they meet Friar Alberigo and Branca Doria.

13-14. Count Ugolino...Archbishop Ruggieri: The two were enemies that joined forces briefly to commit treason, only to have Ruggieri betray Ugolino.

22. the mew: A dark room in which hawks are kept.

28-36. wolf...Gualandi...Sismondi...Lanfranchi: In his dream, Ugolino sees Ruggieri hunting a wolf and cubs (symbolic of Ugolino and his sons) with the aid of the Gualandi, Sismondi, and Lanfranchi, all Ghibelline families. Upon waking he will find that Ruggieri has betrayed him.

79-84. Pisa...Capraia...Gorgona: Dante wishes for the destruction of Pisa, as it is a shame to all those who say 'sì' (that is, Italians), by the islands of Capraia and Gorgona blocking the mouth of the river Arno so the land floods.

88. new Thebes: Pisa is comparable in evil even to Thebes.

91-157. THE TRAITORS AGAINST GUESTS AND HOSTS: The third round of the ninth circle is named Ptolomea after king Ptolemy of Egypt, who allowed his guest Pompey the Great to be killed. These sinners are encased in the ice with only half their head above.

118-120. Brother Alberigo: He was a Guelf who had several of his family killed when he had them over for a meal. The mention of fruit refers to the fact that his call for fruit to be served was the signal to the assassins.

124-126. Ptolomea...Atropos: Alberigo explains that because the sin of treachery against guests and hosts is so evil, a soul may be sent to Hell even before the body dies. This belief was not held by the Church, but rather by some as a popular tradition. Atropos was the Fate who cut the thread of life.

137-147. Ser Branca Doria...Michel Zanche: Branca invited his father-in-law, Zanche (who appears in Canto 22), to eat, and had him killed with the assistance of another family member.

151-157. Genoa: Dante condemns another Italian city, Genoa, where Branca lived.

C ANTO XXXIV

1   "'Vexilla regis prodeunt inferni' in front of us. Look there," my master said, "if you can see him!"

4   Just as how, when there is fog or dark, you can see a windmill turning far in the distance,

7   so I thought that I saw such a shape in the distance; the wind was so great I hid behind my master, because there was nowhere else to hide.

10   Now we stood, and it is with great fear that I repeat it, where there were a great number of men fully encased in ice below us, glimmering through as though the ice were glass.

13   Some were bent over and some appeared to be standing. One here was right side up and one over there was upside down; one was bent over head to toe like a bow.

16   When we had travelled far enough forward that my master was ready to show me that once-beautiful creature,

19   he stopped me and said, "Behold, Dis! See this place; you must have great courage if you hope to go on."

22   At his words I froze completely; how powerless I felt! Do not ask me how I felt, for there are no words to describe it.

I did not die, but I was no longer alive. Dear reader, I   25
challenge you, if you are smart enough, to tell me what I was,
being neither dead nor alive.

This king of this wretched place was encased in ice from the   28
waist down, and I am greater compared to a giant

than giants are to his arms. Just think how large he must be   31
under the ice if the rest of his body is this size as well!

He, if he could have been as good then as he is evil now, and   34
yet still betrayed God, how certainly is he the source of all evil!

And how amazed was I when I saw that he had three faces on   37
his head! The one in front was red,

and the other two joined it at the middle of each shoulder   40
and met at the top of the skull.

The right head was a mix of yellow and white, and the left   43
was black like those who live near the Nile.

From under each head rose two wings, as big as would belong   46
to a bird of his size; yet even ships' sails were not so great as these.

The wings had no feathers, but they looked rather like the   49
wings of a bat, and he beat them so hard that three winds were
given off.

These are the winds that keep all of Cocytus frozen. All his   52
six eyes were crying, and the tears mixed with blood as they fell,

for in each of his three mouths he was chewing up a sinner   55
between his sharp teeth! In this way, they were in eternal
suffering.

But for the man in the front face, the biting was nothing   58
compared to the clawing; at times, all of the skin on his back was
ripped off.

61   "That man that is suffering the most," my master said, "is Judas Iscariot; he is the one that flails his legs, for his head is in Satan's mouth.

64   See the other two, with their heads sticking out? The one in the black face is Brutus; see how he struggles but says nothing.

67   The one there, firm and strong, is Cassius. But see, the night is approaching; let us go…there is nothing more to see here."

70   He motioned me to hold on, and I put my arms around his neck. And when the wings of that beast were apart,

73   he grabbed on to the fur and climbed down through a hole in the ice.

76   When we had reached the thigh of the beast, the guide, straining,

79   turned his head to where his feet had been, and it seemed that he meant to climb up again.

82   "Hold on!" he said, his voice panting with exhaustion. "There are no other paths expect this one to escape Hell."

85   He climbed through an opening in a rock nearby and he seated me there, and then joined me.

88   I looked up, thinking to see Lucifer the same way, but I saw his legs pointing upward.

91   Now if you are so dull that still you cannot figure what point I passed to cause this to happen, how much more confused I was!

94   "Get up," my master said. "The sun is already halfway across the sky, and we have a difficult road ahead of us."

97   We traveled not through a neat passageway, but what was like an animal's path; the floor was uneven and it was dark.

"Before we leave this place, my master," I said when I had   100
stood up, "help me to understand this:

Where is the ice? And why is Lucifer now upside down? And   103
how can the sun be in the middle of the sky when it was night
when we began to descend?"

He replied, "You still think you are near where we descended   106
from, where I climbed the fur of the evil one that bites at the
whole world.

Indeed, you were when we climbed down, but as soon as I   109
turned around, we passed though the center of the earth.

Now we are under the other hemisphere; the sky you are   112
seeing is the one opposite the sky that is above the great deserts
of the earth. It was under that sky

that the sinless man was born and came to suffer and die. We   115
are standing on the bottom of the sphere of Judecca.

When it is evening there, it is morning here, and Satan, who   118
was a ladder for us to descend, is still trapped in the ice.

It is in this hemisphere that he fell from heaven to the earth,   121
and all this land that you see moved to the other hemisphere out
of fright for him;

it is by the same fear that the mountain above us moved up   124
and formed the cavern we came from."

Down at the beginning of this passage there is a small river,   127
that is not seen, but only heard,

that flows through this passage in the path it has eroded in   130
the stone; the path is not too difficult.

133   My guide and I then walked on that road that no men know of that leads from that passage back to the living world, and without even the hope of rest

136   we walked on, he first and with me following. We walked on in darkness until through an opening above I could see the heavens,

139   and once again we could see the stars.

Canto XXXIV Notes

Dante looks ahead and sees what appears to be some structure in the distance, and a great wind fills the whole place. Now they are in a place where the punished souls are completely encased in the ice in various contorted positions. As they progress forward, they find Satan encased in the ice from the waist down. He is a massive beast with three faces and three sets of wings, which give off the cool wind of Cocytus. He is chewing three sinners in his mouths: Judas Iscariot, Brutus, and Cassius. Dante and Virgil climb down Satan's hair through the ice, until they reach the center of the earth. Virgil explains how the falling of Satan from Heaven created the funnel-like structure of Hell. They then travel by a hidden path to the other side of the earth.

1. Vexilla regis prodeunt inferni: Latin for 'the banners of the king of Hell go forward.'

10-69. THE TRAITORS AGAINST MASTERS: This is the final division of Cocytus: Judecca, named after Judas Iscariot, where traitors against masters and lords are punished by being wholly encased in the eternal ice. They can neither move nor speak for all eternity.

20. Dis: In Canto 8, Dis was used as the name of Lower Hell. Here it is used as another name for Satan.

62. Judas Iscariot: The disciple of Jesus who betrayed him to death. Naturally, his punishment is the greatest of any of the humans in Hell.

65-67. Brutus...Cassius: These two friends of Julius Caesar both betrayed him by planning and carrying out his assassination. Dante would have considered the Roman Empire as God's chosen device to spread Christianity throughout the world, and Julius Caesar as God's appointed leader to carry out that work.

103-126. Virgil explains the set of events that caused the formation of Hell. When Satan was cast down from Heaven, all the land on one side of the earth fled to collect in one hemisphere and Satan plunged into the earth, forming the funnel of Hell. Satan's waist is at the center of the earth, so passing through that point causes the direction of gravity to reverse.

115. sinless man: Jesus Christ.

www.ingramcontent.com/pod-product-compliance
Lightning Source LLC
Chambersburg PA
CBHW051821040426
42447CB00006B/305